Publisher's Note

Unusually for any book, what makes these endorsements for *All About Grief* so compelling is that they come from the USA, UK, Africa, India, Asia and Europe and from the widest range of trusted churches, ministries and church networks including: Care for the Family, Focus on the Family, Christ For all Nations (CFAN), Newfrontiers, Salt & Light, David Pawson Trust, Taking Ground, Deliverance Churches and Ground Level.

This book comes highly recommended for all cultures and for all churches.

All About Grief Endorsements

'I urge you to read this remarkable book. It will help you in your own grief, give wise advice as you seek to comfort others and bring the thing we crave for in the darkness of death . . . hope.'

Rob Parsons, OBE, **Founder of Care for the Family**

'Thanks for writing such a tender and truthful book on grief, it acknowledges our unpreparedness for death, the pain of unhelpful "comfort," and the mystery of unanswered prayers. With compassion, it points us to the kind of presence that truly heals and anchors us in God's unfailing promises of hope and nearness.'

Lee Wee Min, Asia Director, **Focus on the Family**

'David Oliver has written an unusual book around a much-neglected subject in the Christian world. What makes it unusual is the fact that it is not the result of theoretical research and pastoral experience, but it comes directly from the hot crucible of personal grief, loss and pain, making it extremely receivable and relevant to all of us.'

Rev. Peter Vandenberg, Executive Vice President,
Christ for all Nations

'Grief afflicts us all sooner or later, and yet surprises many of us by the sudden waves with which it comes, and a depth of pain that we have never known before. We often don't know how to handle our own grief, or how to help others with theirs. This powerful book, written from a deeply painful personal experience, explores the rocky ride of walking through grief, what Christians might expect on this journey, and how we can help and not damage those who have to walk this way. This will be a superb help to many!'

Steve Thomas, Senior Leader, **Salt & Light International & Destinee**

'A deeply honest, compassionate, and hope-filled exploration of grief. Drawing from intense personal loss and much biblical wisdom, David Oliver offers gentle guidance, profound insight and practical comfort for all who walk the painful road of grieving.'

David Rebbettes, Chairman, **David Pawson Ministries**

'Written from tragic personal experience, David Oliver's book All About Grief *is full of counsel for others going through their own journey of grief. It also brings very considerable pastoral wisdom for the benefit of all who are seeking to serve and provide care for others who are experiencing the trauma of grief. I therefore commend All About Grief to you.'*

David Devenish, **Newfrontiers**

'Having read All About Heaven, *I was honoured to be invited to offer an endorsement for* All About Grief. *This is a timely and much-needed book for our generation. Too often, charismatic and evangelical churches – while rightly emphasizing messages of faith, hope and victory – do not give sufficient attention to a thoughtful theology of suffering.*

Forged in the fire of personal grief and bereavement, this book speaks with both authenticity and compassion. It deserves to be read widely, particularly by church leaders and those who care for others in seasons of loss. All About Grief *makes space for the mysteries that surround pain and sorrow, while firmly grounding the reader in trust in a loving and faithful God.'*

Stuart Bell, Founding Pastor, **Alive and Ground Level**

'Having pastored numerous churches for more than thirty years, I have sat with many individuals facing bereavement – how I wish I had had this book then. Birthed in deep pain, it is raw and challenging, yet profoundly instructional and

equipping, unlocking deep emotion. Bravo, David Oliver, bravo! You have expended yourself for us all. This is truly a must-read.'

Steve Oliver, **Regions Beyond**

'With more than 50 years of pastoral ministry behind me, I have encountered the subject of death many times. It is one of the most painful and demanding aspects of fulfilling God's calling to shepherd his people, requiring wisdom, compassion, honesty and sound theology.

David Oliver's book All About Grief *fills a much-needed gap both for those who grieve, and for those entrusted with pastoral care. Every church will, sooner or later, face terminal illness, sudden bereavement, infant loss and the deep complexities of human grief. This book speaks directly and sensitively into those realities.*

I warmly recommend this book to anyone in church leadership as a wise and practical guide. I commend it to those who are walking through the pain of loss and bereavement, and to church members who wish to be better equipped to the inevitable challenges of caring for others in church life. I would also recommend it to anyone seeking answers about the meaning of life and exploring the Christian faith.

This book is an essential resource for the body of Christ.'

David Fellingham, Bible Teacher, Author, Songwriter, **Newfrontiers**

'This book offers a profoundly rich and tender exploration of grief. Emotionally honest and theologically grounded, David brings a remarkable depth of insight to the experience of grief. His words give permission to grieve honestly while pointing gently toward God's sustaining grace. The sensitivity and authenticity with which this book is written will not only bring comfort to those navigating loss it will also equip friends, family and church communities to walk beside them with compassionate sensitivity and understanding.'

Martin Dunkley, Senior Leader, **Taking Ground and New Ground & Tees Valley Community Church**

'As I read this book on grief, I was so moved! I had to stop and reflect in wonder just how much pain Dave and Gill have endured and yet what a help to so many this book will become. "Death has worked in them so that life can work in others." It's real, it's raw at times but it's also full of hope and healing. With the Lord's help, we can make it through such dark valleys and here are a couple whom we can follow and learn from when it's our turn to face such a journey in our lives. I'm so grateful they have written this and I will be giving it to every pastor I work with!'z

Dave Richards, **Salt & Light International Team Coast to Coast (C2C) USA and Salt & Light European Team**

'Many churches do not seem to have a clear theology on death and grief. The only time we think on teaching on these subjects is when there is a death in the church. At such times there a lot of raw emotions. David Oliver has used his personal journey to address the subject of grief in a way that is very helpful".

Bishop JB Masinde, **Deliverance Churches Kenya**

'I was deeply moved by David and Gill's courage in sharing their journey through the devastating loss of their son, Joel. Their vulnerability and honesty drew me in, and while my heart broke with them, I found myself unexpectedly filled with hope – hope rooted in God's sustaining grace even in the darkest valley. This isn't just their story; it's a powerful resource showing us how to walk through loss in a way that honors both the pain and the God who holds us through it.'

Joemon Joseph, Senior Leader, **Gateway Ministries and Salt and Light International**

'This is a brave book! None of us can escape the inevitability of death and grief, yet we often choose to deny or evade it. All About Grief *doesn't allow us to do that. Dave Oliver has not shied away from addressing the deepest of issues. From his own harrowing loss of his son, Joel, to some practical "Do's and Don'ts" we are sensitively led on a journey of facing up to issues such as anger, forgiveness, remarks that hurt and those that comfort and the "Why?" question.*

Don't think that this is a depressing book. It's not. Dave interweaves the deep pain of emotional grief with the sure hope of the Biblical narrative. The reader is left strengthened both in understanding and faith.

David takes us gently but firmly on a journey of the realities of grief and from a place of fearing or ignoring death to daring to look forward to it. I'd encourage everyone to go on that journey. This is one of the most significant and equipping books you will ever read, even if you shed a tear on the way.'

Christine Richards, **Salt & Light European Leadership Team**

'Out of his lived experience, David Oliver pours out profound and validating balm for those who are suffering, and practical insight for those who are called to comfort others.'

Will Horner, Lead Pastor, **Collective Church York**

'When my wife died in 2020 following a long struggle with early onset dementia, I asked myself why no-one had ever prepared me for the deep soul pain of losing my life companion. And now All About Grief *is the companion book I wish I had back then. It is both a great spiritual guide to help Christians navigate the deep soul pain of grief and a brilliant resource for Church leaders. It is highly practical and down to earth in guiding anyone who wishes to know what to do and what to avoid when wanting to comfort people in their grief,*

and how we can process our personal grief while sustaining, if not strengthening, our faith. I highly recommend this book.'

Dr Roger Greene, **Author of Dancing When the Lights Go Out & Deputy CEO at At A Loss**

David Oliver combines searing personal testimony, practical pastoral insight and profound biblical wisdom, in this unique and moving book about the impact of the sudden unexpected loss of his son. I thoroughly recommend this book – it will change you and shape you.

Martin Charlesworth, Senior Leader Christ Central, **Newfrontiers**

ALL ABOUT GRIEF

Comforting those who mourn
Equipping those who care

DAVID OLIVER

malcolm down

PUBLISHING

First published 2026 by Malcolm Down Publishing Ltd.
www.malcolmdown.co.uk

29 28 27 26 6 5 4 3 2 1

British Library Cataloguing in Publication Data
A catalogue record for this book is available from the British Library.

ISBN 978-1-917455-43-5

Cover design by Esther Kotecha
Art direction by Sarah Grace

Printed in the UK

Bottle image by Vecteezy.com

Dedication

To the keeper of the bottle

You have collected all my tears in your bottle

Ps 56.8

2,500 Days and Counting

Acknowledgements and thanks

Whilst I am credited with the writing of this book, that is simply the act of getting words on the page.

Gill Oliver has done much research for this book. Years of reading, searching, viewing and then documenting materials for us to consider together over many hours of painful conversation.

More than that, we have travelled this unchosen journey together for over 2500 days. My closest companion my most faithful friend and my most reliable support.

Thank You

Thanks to Malcolm Down for believing in the book and encouraging me to cross the finish line and thanks to Lydia Jenkins who has helped with pre-launch and launch promotion, as well as proof reading and correcting my error strewn best attempts.

Contents

Introduction: The Phone Call No One Wants 15

1. Death: Inexplicable Unpreparedness 19
2. Dying Well 35
3. Grief and Mourning: A Biblical Perspective 53
4. Grief in Practice 67
5. Anniversaries 87
6. Help That Hurts 101
7. Help That Heals 119
8. Unanswered Prayer, Unanswered Questions and No Regrets 139
9. God's Promises 161
10. No Finish Line: Rebuilding with the Comfort of God 177

Appendix One: Grief Online and the Digital Afterlife 199

Appendix Two: Bereavement Care Checklist 207

All About Grief – Your Church Can Host the Evening Event 215

Free PDF Resources for Readers 219

Bibliography and Resources 221

Endnotes 225

Introduction

The Phone Call No One Wants

This book has been birthed in loss and grief. Joel was our second child of four, and firstborn son. Joel died on 20 December 2018 aged just thirty-eight years and three months.

Just five months earlier in July, Joel had visited our family home and appeared to be in great health. Spending time as a family on the water; chopping down large trees on our property; sharing laughter, meals and board games with joy. During September, he started to get abdominal pains. There was no GP or family doctor diagnosis, just painkillers prescribed in increasing strength. He was then diagnosed with appendicitis and given two weeks on antibiotics. After a week, he had deteriorated, and the family doctor advised attending the Emergency Department where he had multiple scans and a suspected diagnosis of lymphoma.

He was discharged and later readmitted during November. Further investigations began, multiple biopsies were taken and stents inserted. At another point we were given a 'no cancer' diagnosis, and we returned home the four-hour journey from where he and his family lived.

On 28 November Joel called us to say he did have cancer, but they still didn't know where. It would most likely be inoperable. He didn't want us to travel the long distance to be with him at that time, as he imagined it would likely be a long haul with extensive treatments.

A few days later he called again to say through tears that he had been given from a few weeks up to six months to live and would the family come up to be close by? As a family in various permutations, we travelled up to County Durham and with his wife, Joanna, we cared for him the best we knew in the hospital, taking shifts day and night so he wouldn't be alone. During that time, we had multiple breath-taking shocks, great highs and unimaginable lows. Joel was eventually diagnosed with Stage 4 bowel cancer.

Our family had to watch Joel – our precious, previously very healthy son in his absolute prime – reduced to a man often in excruciating pain, receiving brutal interventions, battered and bruised and scarred from treatments and from those interventions.

The evening before he died, at Joel's request, we sat with him while the oncology consultant told him the medical team had agreed to withdraw any further treatment or support and were going to let him die. The following day at 12.57 with the whole family around him, Joel took his last breath.

From the initial shock of the doctor's final pronouncement, seventeen life-changing, exhausting days later and Joel was safe in the arms of Jesus.

I love all my family equally and at the same time Joel was my best friend, in part because he was a co-labourer in church and a co-labourer at work. We would sail together, enjoy wine together and do the great outdoors together. We would talk to each other on the phone every day, email every day. We had grand business growth plans which we initiated and then implemented together. The loss has left all of us reeling.

After Joel's death there were the inevitable questions including the obvious one: Why? That question I've observed over the years rarely gets answered. Actually, a different question became important to me: What can I do that I could not do before? What should I do that I wouldn't have considered before? So, I committed, as one small step in my response, to write the book *All About Heaven*[1] and from the response to that book, and subsequent evening events around the world that have reached many thousands, I have set about writing this book, *All About Grief*.

Writing is not new to me. This is my fifteenth book and yet the writing journey has been unlike anything else I have written or tried to write. I said to my wife, Gill, 'It's like a baby that has been in my womb for years, not months. It's wriggled around, it's kicked me and bruised me, it's made me sick, it's had me in tears and now here it comes slithering out all bloody and yelling at anyone who will take notice.'

Most books have only taken me two weeks to get to a first draft after the research. This one has taken years. I could only manage two hours per day and definitely only a few days a week. Why? Because true grief is attritional, and writing about it is not cathartic; quite the reverse.

After Joel died, there was a whole range of extreme emotions. And they were off the scale, different to anything I had experienced before. Sharp shards of white-hot pain that unbidden would pierce the innermost recesses of my soul, and at times cause almost involuntary howls of grief. At other times the emptiness, the loss of all the dreams, all the plans, and above it all, the loss of someone who loved us so deeply and who we loved like crazy.

It's seven years on now. We have had the unwelcome honour and privilege of being initiated as members into the club no one wants to join, walking with God through suffering, death, dying, grief and mourning and in it all discovering God's hand, God's ways and God's compassion.

We've been encouraged by friends, pastors and readers to put our journey of grief into print. Not as some kind of template or checklist for those who grieve, but to open up conversations that deal honestly with the things that rocked us; the things that helped us cling on when we felt we might fall over the precipice, and the things that ultimately enabled us over time to find our place in God's New Different Season for us.

Chapter One

Death: Inexplicable Unpreparedness

Most of us, if not all of us, have lost a family member or friend. Some have been through the pain of losing a spouse. Others will have lost a mum or dad. Many of us will have lost a grandparent; some will have a lost a brother or sister. It will be the case that some have had the loss of miscarriage, stillbirth, or a precious life 'born sleeping'. Some, like Gill and me, have lost a son or daughter.

Few of us have ever been taught about these things with clarity and confidence; and in the deep pain, the grief and the confusion, there are all kinds of questions, aren't there?

This book is written with the hope that we can help everyone navigate their way through the inevitable journey from death to grief and mourning, and into that, some practical thoughts and some dependable scriptures. And the first place we start is with our preparedness for death.

The solid bet!

Benjamin Franklin made the point, 'In this world nothing can be said to be certain, except death and taxes'.[1] Death is what Derek Prince calls the 'universal appointment'.[2] It's a solid bet. It will happen to us all. It's a dead cert. The scripture clarifies that one person out of one dies. Old or young, millionaire or penniless, homeless, alone or in the bosom of the family, one thing is sure, inevitable, certain and without any question – we will die. Unless Jesus returns, every one of us will die.

When I go sailing to a new port or a new destination, I can spend hours, sometimes even days, planning, researching and preparing for a short voyage. And yet given the 100 per cent certainty of death, isn't it surprising that we talk so little about it, we plan so little for it – the most important journey of all time. We live as if it is the most unlikely thing ever to happen. There is, in the Christian community, an almost inexplicable unpreparedness.

Our society is on the run from death – we are not even supposed to use the word 'death'. Passed on, passed away, sorry you've lost him. If death is the one thing that is certain for every man or woman on the planet; why is it the topic most feared, most avoided and least talked about? God doesn't view it like that. God's desire is for us to have a healthy understanding of death and in fact, far more than that. It's been said we cannot live well unless we die well.

I was travelling with a friend recently, chatting about this, and he quoted the common view which is that *death is something that happens to someone else.* Honestly that's how many of us as Christians live. I'm not disparaging anyone, it's just we have had so little preparation in our church life thus far. Contrast that with the Jewish view where death is seen, talked about and experienced by all the family as an integral part of life.

One of my Jewish friends put it this way: We live lives with the inevitability that we will have a demise; every one of us will leave this earth. And yet nothing explains the sudden nature of it. Author Roger Greene says:

> The reality of death at some point in our lives doesn't diminish the pain and the grief, but it helps to see the pain and grief as a natural part of life rather than an aberration that has to be hidden or denied. There is no shame in grief. It is part of what it means to be human and now that I've experienced grievous loss, I understand life as incomplete without it.[3]

Old Testament scripture helps us pragmatically here. Ecclesiastes reminds us there is 'a time to be born and a time to die', and continues, 'It is better to go to a house of mourning than to go to a house of feasting, for death is the destiny of everyone; the living should take this to heart . . .

The heart of the wise is in the house of the mourning, the heart of fools in the house of pleasure.'[4]

Paul gives another helpful view where in the New Testament Christian experience, death and the resurrection that follows is of 'first importance'.[5] In Hebrews, Paul unpacks six truths which he talks of as the first principles of Christ and a foundation. Two of those six have to do with death and what follows, namely resurrection and judgement.[6]

So, it is not an issue to be afraid of or to bypass, it is by definition at the heart of one of the six foundational blocks and is of first importance. Primary: Number one. All that suggests this is not a topic to be avoided or to shrink back from; it's a dead cert, it's a universal appointment and it's the only doorway available to the best of God on offer. Death is another subject on which you and I are called to have a different attitude. Of course, we grieve when someone dies. But Paul says we should not 'grieve like the rest, who have no hope'.[7] We've said it already but it bears repeating; no one can live well unless they die well. Death is another subject on which the Bible has a dramatically alternative view. Many people see only a *hopeless end*, but you and I have an *endless hope*. Remind and 'encourage each other with these words'[8] – you and I are called to have a different attitude.

What happens when we die?

This question must be asked thousands of times every day. A hundred and five people die every minute. That's more than 3,000 by the time you have finished this chapter!

As we all know, at the moment of death, certain physical processes stop – breathing stops, heart stops, circulation stops, hair can carry on growing for a while! Then the process of decay comes. If a human being is only a body, then by definition that must be the end.

The scientist Einstein developed the first law of thermodynamics. It doesn't agree! Neither energy (soul and spirit) nor matter (body) can be destroyed. They can be transformed into other forms, but they cannot be annihilated.[9]

This is attributed to Burris Jenkins: 'No single atom in creation can go out of existence according to scientists; it only changes in form.'[10]

Death is not the winner because death is not the end. Death's victory and the sting in its tail does not apply to those who love God.[11] Physical death does not mean annihilation; it is not the end; it is in fact the liberating door to the very best of God which lies beyond the grave.

The Bible puts it this way: 'Dust returns to the ground it came from, and the spirit returns to God who gave it.'[12] Death is the moment of separation between body and spirit. Two things intimately entwined, which we have not seen separated before, becoming separated. When

Jesus famously turned to the dying thief, his statement lay a clear foundation for us: 'Today you will be with me in paradise.'[13] The Master was making it clear, the last breath on the cross, the next breath with Him in a place called Paradise.

People said to us, 'Sorry that you have lost Joel.' Gill said, 'No! He is not lost; we know where he is. We have placed him into the safe arms of Jesus.' The imagery, the metaphor in Gill's mind, was important. In a similar way to the way the midwife had first handed this newly born son into her arms, Gill was placing this same son into the safe arms of Jesus. Certain he was not lost, and confident of his place, his location, his being in the next realm, the next life. His last breath with us, his family, his next breath in reality in the presence of Jesus.

For the Christian, death is different, it must be different, it has to be different, it really is different! We haven't lost Joel; we have placed him safely in the arms of Jesus. Death is not a brick wall, not a dark end, not an impenetrable block at the end of our life's tunnel; it's a doorway to the greatest adventure of all time. It's the journey home after a long time away. It's a doorway to a world that's better than the best we have ever had, or could ever imagine.

None of us relish the thought of dying. Seeing loved ones die in some trauma or from a short or long illness is shocking to us. Instinctively we recoil. 'This should not be' is our normal and natural reaction; and in that very response we find echoes of God's Eden stirring. We find genetic echoes of eternal life and at the deepest level, we know death was never the intent of God. So of course, we recoil and often find ourselves gasping with shock and pain in the middle of it all.

Wonderful to learn then that the Bible gives at least five metaphors, tender, illuminating, caring metaphors, to explain what happens at death:

A Shepherd's Tent or a Weaver's Loom

Isaiah tells us:

> I said, In the middle of my days
> I must depart . . .
> My dwelling is plucked up and removed from me
> like a shepherd's tent;
> like a weaver I have rolled up my life;
> he cuts me off from the loom;[14]

It's a great metaphor from everyday life, originally written as a poem of thanksgiving by King Hezekiah, who was facing imminent death, as God grants him fifteen years more life. This body I inhabit is taken down and packed away like a camper's tent. Like a weaver, I've rolled up the beautifully woven fabric of my life as God cuts me free of the loom, and at day's end sweeps up the scraps and pieces.

As a camper, my tent is a temporary dwelling, not my home. The weaver's fabric on the loom is never the end itself – the fabric is designed for another place and another function; it is meant to be set somewhere else, doing something else.

A collapsing tent

Our bodies are described by the Apostle Paul as a 'tent' in which we live. He says that 'if the earthly tent we live in is destroyed, we have a building from God, an eternal house in heaven, not built by human hands'.[15] Tents deteriorate with the ageing process of life, the weather and storms that they face, and when we die, the tent of our body dismantles or disintegrates. It's as if our body is just a suit of clothes worn by the real person. The Bible talks about the outward man decaying and the inner man getting stronger.[16] I've heard various speakers over the years effectively describing a cemetery as no more than a cloakroom where we put aside the old clothes we have worn.

In Philippians and 2 Timothy, Paul enlarges the picture by suggesting all the delights of a long-delayed homecoming. This is the last of his letters.

A longed-for departure

Paul talks of death possibly in the context of the sailing of a ship. In a familiar passage, he says, 'I desire to depart and be with Christ.'[17] In 2 Timothy, written when he sensed his time of death was close, he describes it beautifully as the time of his 'departure',[18] using a specific word meaning either time for him to 'strike camp' or to 'weigh anchor'.

You'll recall his occupation as a tentmaker, and his travelling, often by sea, on his missionary journeys. Either way, this established tent manufacturer, this seasoned ocean sailor, is using a picture drawn from his trade or a common but memorable moment from one of his many sailing trips.

In either case, the meaning is the same. All the hassle, the lack of comforts and the discomforts, deprivations of camping and the homesickness most of us endure after an extended period in a foreign land are now past, with the joy of going home implicit.

Falling asleep

This description has caused some confusion over the years, and it is important for us to understand it. The Bible uses the phrase 'fallen asleep' referring quite clearly to those who have died. Because of that, some believe that when we die, we stay in limbo – an unconscious state – until the return of Jesus. Some preachers have taught 'soul sleep'. In other words, when we die, we enter a kind of spiritual coma, asleep in a non-physical body until we wake up to the sound of the last trumpet. There are many problems with this view, not least as it causes unnecessary distress to some, confusion or uncertainty to others, and can rob us of any desire to leave this earth. Interestingly, both Jesus and Paul used the term. Both of them in different ways made it clear that it referred to the body, not the spirit. In other words, it is the body that has gone to sleep until resurrection day.

I love the thought of drifting off when my head hits the pillow: sometimes just the look of the bed and the soft lighting appeals so strongly early in the evening, I have to resist the urge to lie down there and then! I know some struggle with sleep, but for many of us, we look forward to the moment of switching off and then switching back on ready to go for a new day, a new adventure when we wake up in the morning.

Falling asleep points us to the reality that death in the body is temporary, not permanent – we do wake up – and equally makes the point that we need be no more worried about death than we would be about falling asleep.

In Luke 16, Jesus tells the story of Lazarus and the rich man. Lazarus is in paradise, or by Abraham's side, and the rich man is in conscious torment, his spirit imprisoned. Neither of these are in any way asleep. They are fully conscious and are talking, feeling, seeing and hearing. In the Gospels, Elijah and Moses appear at the transfiguration with Jesus.[19] Whatever else we might deduce, we can certainly see that they were very much alive, engaged and conscious.

When Stephen is being stoned to death he cries out, "'Lord Jesus, receive my spirit.' Then he fell on his knees and cried out, "Lord, do not hold this sin against them." When he had said this, he fell asleep.'[20] It is virtually identical to the prayer that Jesus prayed on the cross to the Father[21] and Jesus certainly did not sleep. Stephen has seen him standing at the right hand of the Father.[22] Spirits don't sleep. This is clear from the story of Jairus' daughter: 'Her spirit *returned,* and at once she stood up.'[23] It can't return if it was asleep. It was her body that was asleep and her body that stood up at the returning of her spirit.

In a number of ways, Paul makes it even clearer. He says, 'Therefore we are always confident and know that as long as we are at home in the body we are away from the Lord. . . . We are confident, I say, and would prefer to be away from the body and at home with the Lord.'[24] In Philippians, Paul says, 'For to me, to live is Christ and to die is gain. If I am to go on living in the body, this will mean fruitful labour for me. Yet what shall I choose? I do not know! I am torn between the two: I desire to depart and be with Christ, which is better by far; but it is more necessary for you that I remain in the body.'[25]

To reframe this, we can see:

- 'at home in the body' we are 'away from the Lord';
- 'away from the body and at home with the Lord';
- 'to live is Christ and to die is gain';
- 'I desire to depart and be with Christ, which is better by far'.

Going Home

These four statements can only be made if Christians are immediately in the presence of the Lord. Notice, too, the notion that what lies ahead is truly 'home'. Paradise or 'at home with the Lord' are both phrases used by Jesus, John and Paul to describe the present heaven for the Christian who dies. I often tell people that, 'I am going home inside.' I long for my true home. Scripture tells us this world is not our home; we are aliens, exiles looking forward to our true home. And if we could see it, most of us are homesick for our true home.[26]

Jesus also said, 'I [go] to prepare a place for you.'[27] That's a home designed by Jesus, a place he has purpose built for you and for me, and I can't wait for that next home. *Grand Designs* or *Amazing Interiors*, eat your heart out! I believe in eternal life, I believe that heaven is 'better by far' and I believe that for me 'to live is Christ and to die is gain'; to die is better. To die is the doorway to an even better life and I can't wait. I love the life I have here. I love Gill, my family, my home, my work, but I know the next life is exponentially better. And if I really do believe that, it makes handling suffering, pain and grief so much easier in the here and now.

And wonderfully, right here, Scripture takes responsibility and offers rock-solid hope, shaping our thoughts and shaping our perspectives.

Our first scripture in this context is, 'Precious in the sight of the LORD is the death of his faithful servants. Truly I am your servant, LORD; I serve you just as my mother did; you have freed me from my chains.'[28]

I don't know what chains the psalmist was thinking of, but I suspect it included unnecessary fear of death and a wrong view of death. God says death is precious for those that belong to him. God is speaking to us and saying, 'Don't view it negatively, because I don't. View it as precious, view it as glorious, view it as highly valued.' 'Precious' is a word I would normally use relationally with Gill or with one of our children, usually at times of great closeness or affection. This is at the heart of this statement: it's God's affectionate heart saying, 'You're coming home and I love you.' This is a precious moment.

In some of His last words to his disciples Jesus said, 'I am going away . . . If you loved me, you would be glad that I am going . . .'[29] Jesus himself longed to be going home.

Remembering that moment and, I suspect, deeply impacted by those words, decades later the Apostle John, nearing his own 'departure', wrote, 'Then I heard a voice from heaven say, "Write this: blessed are the dead who die in the Lord from now on".'[30] Blessed because we are going home.

Free from fear

Satan designed death as the greatest horror, the icy hand, the fear-filled journey to doom, the dark valley of foreboding. But God says, 'It is precious in my sight'.[31] These are victory words. I was deeply moved by a story told by Nobel Prize winner and holocaust survivor Elie Wiesel of the little girl in the sealed cattle car en route eventually to the gas chambers of Auschwitz, a little girl who, hugging her grandmother, whispered, 'Don't be afraid, don't be sorry to die . . . I'm not.'[32] She was seven, that little girl who went to her death without fear, without regret.

It has been suggested that ultimately all our fears are related to the fear of death. In setting us free from death and the fear of death, Jesus has enabled you and me to be set free from all our other fears.

The writer of Hebrews says that Jesus tasted 'death for everyone'[33] so that by 'embracing death, taking it into himself, he destroyed the Devil's hold on death and freed all who cower through life, scared to death of death.'[34]

Mother Teresa reflected on this in several comments including her Nobel Prize speech. She puts it this way, 'Heaven is our home. People ask me about death and whether I look forward to it and I answer, "Of course", because I am going home.'[35]

Death reveals what life tries to ignore and camouflages with busyness and preoccupations. Death reveals that heaven is real and I really want to be there. This takes a moment to grasp, but this too can be liberating. Tens of thousands have read the book *All About Heaven* or watched the event by the same name, and one of the most common reactions is joy at what lies ahead and a newfound longing to be there. Paul was so utterly enthralled by what he saw in paradise he wrote, 'I desire to depart and be with Christ, which is better by far'.[36]

The best of God lies beyond the grave

And here's the obvious statement. The only way to get to heaven is through death. If Adam and Eve had eaten of the tree of life, they would have been immortalised in their sinful condition; they would never have qualified for the heaven that God wanted them to enjoy. Eden paradise would have been lost to them eternally, forever living without the possibility of transformation with all the consequences of their sin.

Following the Fall when all seemed lost and dark, God gave the gift of death; the ability to exit this life and arrive safely at the jaw-dropping best of God and life to come. Death, though it appears to be humanity's greatest enemy, would in the end prove to be its greatest friend. Think then of how utterly powerless death is.

Chapter Two

Dying Well

As I write this chapter in the UK, we are in the middle of a heated national debate around so-called assisted dying and the topic has been forced into the national consciousness. This book is not intended to address that debate, but nonetheless, it has brought the notion of the fear of dying and questions about how we die into national conversation.

People live and people die; can we do both well without regret?[1]

On one level, no one really wants to think about suffering or talk about it, and I get that. In fact, for some reading this book, your loved one may well have died instantaneously in an accident or from a heart attack and this chapter may not be for you. However, for most of us, dying can be a very unpleasant prospect to contemplate. There is inevitable and understandable apprehension over pain, treatments and interventions. Concern over outcomes is a stark and ongoing reality. On a practical level, by and large in the West when it comes to a terminal diagnosis, pain is managed well. That's not a guarantee and it's not an absolute; but generally, our end-of-life care does handle that well.

However, in the same way that everyone handles grief differently and in the same way that grief pushes its unwelcome way into our lives differently, so too there are variations in the manner of dying that impact both the one suffering and the family and friends who accompany their loved one in that journey of suffering.

The dying challenge gets further compounded because there is the one going through suffering and also the family and friends who accompany their loved one on that journey of suffering. And then there are deaths that are sudden, instant, shockingly unexpected and that too is different.

A theology of dying

Old Testament thought emphasises the naturalness of death as part of the cycle of life. Ecclesiastes says, 'There is . . . a time to be born and a time to die',[2] encouraging acceptance of life's impermanence. And the earliest biblical insights into death and dying are found in the book of Job.

Then from the thinking developed in the New Testament, I want to suggest that there is something in our death that not only opens the door to heaven, wonderful and desirable as that is; but that following the Fall and the loss of the Tree of Life, dying itself is part of God's purpose in our lives. I say that with a great deal of trepidation, not certain that I like the sound of my own words here!

Paul may have had something like this in mind with two scriptures: '. . . it is my eager expectation and hope that I will not be at all ashamed, but that with full courage now as always Christ will be honoured in my body, whether by life or by death. For to me to live is Christ, and to die is gain.'[3]

Paul expresses his desire that Christ be honoured or glorified, in both life and death. His attitude reflects a life entirely dedicated to God – right to the very end: 'For none of us lives for ourselves alone, and none of us dies for ourselves alone. If we live, we live for the Lord; and if we die, we die for the Lord. So, whether we live or die, we belong to the Lord.'[4]

Our very identity in Christ continues in death. This surrender – living and dying to the Lord – is an act of glorifying God with our whole being.

Pope Francis 'offered his suffering'. He often spoke about transforming personal suffering into acts of love and solidarity. He reminded the faithful that 'even in the most painful of our sufferings, we are never alone. The prayer of Jesus is with us'.[5]

In his teachings, Pope Francis often reflected on the transformative power of suffering when united with prayer and compassion.

Maybe these small indications from scripture will give us the courage we need to know that 'I will never leave you or forsake you'[6] includes our suffering and dying.

One friend wrote these words a month before she died:

> I'll not look back but hold onto your hand. Waiting on you, Lord, is the task that I must do from the place of my confinements. There my words are tested true, like the soul of a favourite child found resting close to you, nestled warm. My eyes remain on you, for the battles rage round me and my strength indeed is small. Storm clouds brew within me. On your name I now have called. Mercy gently rains upon me washing all my fears below.
>
> I see your Son, he's standing by your side interceding for me faithful as the anointed one. Gaining new strength in my weakness I now stand. Once a dying flame of fire, I feel my wick now found because your spirit has forged the way now to the promised land.[7]

How we die matters

Of course, I am biased, but Joel's manner of dying was, in my mind at least, a masterclass of victorious Christian departure. I have said many times if I could be half the man my son was in his dying then I would be a man indeed. The whole family was there when as Dad, with the privilege and responsibility of last words, I pronounced, 'Joel David, you have run the race, fought the fight, there is now a crown of life ready and waiting for you.'[8] He drew his last breath and was gone. The peace of God was present in a very substantial manner. Doctors and nurses came in and out, with some shedding tears on their own and with us. I don't believe they had ever witnessed a dying like this one.

Joel's courageous response to treatment, his acute presence of mind, his thoughtfulness and kindness towards others, family, his staff, his church leadership team, the hospital staff, was exemplary. His intent was to prepare himself and each of us for the outcomes we would face. It was very moving on the penultimate day, how he talked about having no right to life or death; and yet in that same breath, articulated how he still hoped for healing so he could dance on the streets and make sense of it all.

The danger of healing expectations

In the charismatic and evangelical world there can be a subtle pressure which implies victorious Christianity means healing is for everyone, and for every sickness. Hope for healing and prayer for healing can add to unnecessary stresses and strains at a time of suffering. I have seen families feeling like their faith is deficient or feeling the need to pray more, even fast more and, in the process, add an unmanageable weight to their already demanding experience. I have seen people told that it's their lack of faith that's the problem. The crushing weight of that on top of grief and pain is cruel.

And yes, I do believe in prayer for healing; I do believe in the injunction to call for the elders and be anointed and I do believe the prayer of faith will save the sick.[9] And I also believe 'there is a time to die' and it is absolutely the case that Jesus really does 'hold the keys of death'.[10] No one else gets to open that lock; not the healing ministry, not faith or fasting, not even the medical profession. He holds those keys. Fact.

Joel postured us and talked about each of us needing to find peace with cancer. 'You will have questions,' he said, 'that will not be answered this side of heaven, and you will need to make peace with that.' In Chapter Eight, we unpack this more fully but because it intrudes on the process of dying it is potentially helpful to get a perspective here. So, yes of course, we pray for healing and yes, we will get the church and the elders to pray. But we will also learn from the Apostle Paul who prayed three times and then without his answer was able to lean into the truth that 'my grace is sufficient in your weakness'.[11] Focusing only on an insistence on healing can easily rob us of the powerful enabling and empowering grace that we could otherwise lean into to help us die well.

Better than life?

My father died when I was twenty-one. I had the privilege of nursing him with my mum. We had fought over six long months for his recovery. We had prayed and fasted for his healing, and then the end came close. I remember going through stages of anger, sadness, fighting the seeming injustice of it all. The night he died, I was sleeping downstairs, not far away from his bed. He actually died while we were both asleep. When I woke up, I heard no breathing and looked across at my first sight of death.

In the shock of it all, in my nervous unpreparedness, something happened. I found myself kneeling at the foot of the bed on which he lay, sensing the presence of God and his angels. This was not me trying to be good or to be spiritual, this just happened. I found myself singing a worship song. It is a scripture that at the time the church was adapting as a praise song: 'Your loving kindness is better than life, My lips shall praise You. Thus will I bless You . . .'[12] Somehow God breathed his perspective into my heart and mind, right at the time when I needed it most.

His lovingkindness really is better than life. He said it; we can trust it. When a loved one is dying, everything in us wants them to be healed, to live, to get better. It's because their life right there, right then is the most important thing in our minds, and of course, it's understandable. But as we explore this, we begin to see and maybe believe that God's purpose for our loved ones and for us is faultless and not a mistake. His lovingkindness, however we feel right now, maybe for many years to come, is going to work all things together for good,[13] it really is. His lovingkindness will always be greater than life.

Making preparation

One of the reasons for making space for this chapter is that we have learned that people have very different preferences and expectations; the one who is suffering and those who walk the journey alongside. There is no checklist of 'rights and wrongs' and no standard to achieve. But it can be helpful to have some possibilities to consider, perhaps acting as a catalyst for conversations. Some of these practical reflections may resonate, others may not; either way, maybe it will help in highlighting things that may be important to you and your loved ones.

Words that matter

I found myself reflecting on the lasting value of Joel's words. In his last days Joel was outstandingly thoughtful and caring to us all, and he took care to say things that would make a difference, words that would have beneficial impact, words that would help us navigate the uncharted unchosen days that would follow.

He told us all in different ways how much he loved us. He made sure he eyeballed us and told us, 'No regrets.' He thought through the inevitable pressures that would follow and told us, 'You'll get some things right and some things wrong, that's OK.' How often Gill and I have leaned into the shelter of those words over the past seven years.

He instructed us towards the end to be sure to regularly read a passage in the Bible known as 'the armour of God', which is found in Ephesians 6; not certain why, but he seemed aware as he said, 'You will need it.' Seven years on it has become doubly significant.

His words surround us. Over the years he had taken to writing pretty much anywhere. When he gave gifts, he would write on the wrapping for sure, but sometimes on the gift itself. We have words written in indelible marker on the inside door of our best dining room cupboards. There are words in our understairs cupboard. Preparing for Christmas meals, Gill found a message written in the Delia Smith recipe book. On a picture in our bedroom his words reside. On my boat, every time I lift the cover to my instruments, I read 'Hi Dad' written in indelible marker. Every time I sail, every time, it either prompts a salty tear, or a smile, or both.

His words could be found in the most unlikely places. Every year we worked together with a team at a big event in a national exhibition and conference centre in London. He had amazing vision; each year creating one of the most outstanding stands in the venue, running a large team of demonstrators and sales staff. Each year he would also arrange for me to have multiple speaking sessions and keynotes. We would have a blast each day working together, and then memorable team evenings out in stunning locations. Every year he and I shared the hotel room. In the last year, he had already begun to feel a little unwell, and to my surprise he left the event early. When I got back to our hotel room, he had written in shaving foam on the mirror 'Thanks, Dad'. Thankfully I took a photo and now of course it's a treasured memory.

From his hospital bed he arranged for many of us to get gifts. One gift he had arranged for me I knew would be the last thing I would ever open. And in fact, it was over two years before I could bring myself to commit to unwrapping the package. Some months before the opening, I had to put my signature to a document that sold a business he and I had worked in together for more than a decade. It was meant to be a dream deal that would enable us to do all kinds of good things. However, with his departure it was a dream that could not be realised. I'm not absolutely sure why, but the finality of this moment, the loss of this 'Father & Son' dream was one of the hardest moments on my journey.

Opening the gift, I found an outstandingly beautiful pen and pencil writing set. He had wanted some words inscribed but there wasn't enough room so with the gift box came an inscribed card, 'To Dad, For all the deals we would have done'. Two plus years on and his thoughtful words brought light into a moment of deep darkness. Tears yes, but healing words.

I am deeply grateful for a son who knew the value of words and left his family with words that have made a lasting impact.

Nothing left unsaid

It's also so important that wherever possible there's nothing left unsaid. If things need to be put right, then in tenderness do your best. Reach back into good memories and relive them. Make sure love and honour are communicated as best you can.

One reader wrote these words:

> As sad as it was to observe my husband's decline, the fact he had very good palliative care at home was very helpful. In the period before his cancer spread, we had time to be very honest, and living one day at a time took on fresh importance. The fact I don't have to carry secrets about the past is helping me to have courage. I used to read a little bit from the Bible each evening by his bed. Even when it got to the point he wasn't listening, it helped me.[14]

Three days before Joel departed, not knowing it was that close, but wanting to say something good and encouraging I sent an email:

> Hi son, just want to say again and again and again and again I love you deeply and am so proud of your solid manly responses to daily pain, trauma and disappointment. I wish I could do more, pray more, take more, heal more, be more. My world, the world, is such a better place for having you. Try and sleep some tonight dearest sweetest son, take the meds they suggest if you can, and let the meds do their job.
>
> From your super proud, super loving, super grateful Dad

Pictures and recordings

Every family experience will be different, but with Joel and with his agreement we took pictures. We also had audio recordings and if there's one thing I've learned from grief it's to take pictures. Take pictures of everything everywhere of every single person you love and every single memory you want to keep; because at some point that's all you'll have left and it's the only way you'll feel close to them. I've spoken to countless grieving families not once have I heard anyone say 'we have too many pictures'. On the other hand, I have heard from people wishing deeply that they had more pictures. My encouragement is to make the time to take pictures, to be intentional about it. With our smartphones, it's never been easier and it's easy too; deleting what we don't want to keep with the touch of a finger on our phones.

Family experiences in dying

Inevitably it was Joel's wife, Joanna, who carried the huge weight of responsibility in her outstanding care of Joel through the multiple hospital and doctor procedures and interventions. In the last few weeks, between us as a family and with some friends, we cared for Joel in hospital 24/7. And just in case you are wondering, this is not normal in the UK. The staff were great, although at times a little nonplussed. We moved into the hospital and operated a shift system so that he was never alone. It was most definitely the best care for him. We are a medical family, and I would never recommend this for anyone else; it was simply what was right for us to do and was definitely the best for Joel. He had asked for someone from his family or circle of close friends to be with him as, ideally, he didn't want to be alone, as I mentioned before.

All this, of course, had its challenges. The long days and nights and trying to fit normal life into the plan was challenging, and there was the maelstrom of emotions, what I have come to see as a cocktail of multiple shocks – grief and pain – all condensed into a short timeframe. Sometimes we had no chance to process one shock before another would be unleashed.

It was during this process that we became acquainted with the cat flap.

The cat flap

Sitting in the hospital every day, it was common for us to find ourselves wondering how all this came to be. It seemed so surreal and would regularly unleash a rollercoaster of unimaginable proportions. What will the future hold? Life can never be the same, and what does that mean? Just three months ago, Joel was chain-sawing trees in our garden and another day, sailing onboard *Cool Runnings* with the family to all intents and purposes a strong and healthy man. We love the hundreds of memories like these that come cascading in, doing their best to heal the grief. However, at the same time memories of the various treatments taking place would open up what Joel called 'the cat flap'. Sometimes you can choose to open it up and let grief out and it's reasonably under control. Other moments, without warning a memory or an action pushes that cat flap open and intense grief comes pouring out, taking everyone by surprise.

It became very clear early on that unbridled emotion was unhelpful, and in this context 'the cat flap' became worth its weight in gold. If there was to be an unavoidable communication about treatments or outcomes, then we would be told this was likely a cat flap moment. More frequently, if Gill or I wanted to share a memory or discuss something likely to be difficult, we would learn to ask, 'Can you handle a cat flap moment?' Or we might ask one another, 'Would it help to have a cat flap moment?'

It was a helpful, gentle way of asking for permission or offering permission.

When words can't be spoken or prayed out loud

We were blessed with Joel in that he was able to communicate verbally right to the end. For many others this is not the case. With the death of my dad, there were moments when he was no longer able to communicate, and I received counsel to read scripture to pray and to continue to talk as if he could communicate. Having subsequently been involved in scores of pastoral situations with other families sitting with them and their loved ones, I can testify that communicating with the departing loved one brings peace into the situation and more often than not is accompanied by the tiniest of observable responses.

A reader recently wrote this:

> And so our family and my son's family asked [the dying person] if she would pray. They would take turns putting their hand in hers and when she was done with her thinking the prayer, she put her hand down and then she put the next one up. She prayed for each one of the family just before she passed.

Privacy and support

When it comes to health issues, especially when it's a potentially terminal sickness, lots of families and individuals quite wisely want to be able to control the flow of information and are therefore naturally very cautious, guarding what gets into the public domain. This is especially critical with what ends up on social media. In our case we were at the end of our emotional and physical capacity, and it's an understatement to say we were all desperately in need of prayer support and encouragement. We had a hugely supportive church family so, we would send out a prayer update from time to time to a selected group and every time remind them that this was confidential and not to be shared on social media.

We also had one trusted person in our church that took responsibility for the communication and fielded any enquiries. That way we never got bothered, nor did we face any unhelpful intrusion. Nor did any detail find its way onto social media. However, even with all this care we still missed one email which went to a close friend of Joel's and caused unnecessary pain.

What I can tell you is that as a family, we were only able to cope as well as we did in Joel's final weeks because of the many Christians around the world in scores of churches who faithfully prayed for us day and night.

Dying well includes leaning into your faith and leaning into the support network that church uniquely offers, but being aware of the potential pitfalls in communication.

Chapter Three

Grief and Mourning: A Biblical Perspective

We have looked at death from a biblical perspective but does Scripture hold helpful clues for the challenging journey of grief and mourning, for those left behind?

My views are coloured by experience. As I mentioned earlier, when I was twenty-one years old, I nursed my dad until he went to be with the Lord. It was my first-ever experience of death and my very first sight of a dead person and that dead person was my dad. I will never forget the moment because my mum and I had prayed fervently, others had prayed, there had been fasting and of course there was huge sadness and a parallel disappointment.

Much later in life we were able to ensure my mother was cared for until her peaceful death, and we nursed Gill's mother in our home until she died. I tell you these stories because they influence my understanding of Jesus' words, as I will make clear in a moment.

The experience of these three deaths, all close, all family, were one thing, and the promised comfort of Jesus in

Matthew[1] was also one thing, but the death of my son Joel was on a different level, beyond the pain of anything I could have ever imagined.

With Gill's mum and dad and my mum, there were tears, but they were tinged with relief and the intensity of mourning was light because they were all past their three score years and ten[2] and all wanted to go home.

With Joel, it was different. From the initial shock of the doctor's pronouncement, seventeen life-changing, exhausting days later and Joel was safe in the arms of Jesus. For Joel, of course, it's 'better by far', better than the best he had ever experienced on earth . . . wonderful as his life was. It really is 'better by far' – but, and it's a huge BUT . . .

What about the pain and turbulence for those of us left behind? As mentioned earlier Joel was my best friend, a co-labourer in church and a co-labourer at work. We would sail together, enjoy wine together and do the great outdoors together. We would talk to each other on the phone every day, email every day. Every day! Writing this chapter in my office today, he would have called to see what I would be sharing and he would likely have prayed for me and you. The loss has left all of us reeling and the levels of grief our family has been through is:

- off the chart
- off the scale
- beyond anything I could have ever contemplated.

And yes, we do still feel it seven years on.

As a family, each in our own unique and varied ways, we have had to live with and learn to process the mental, emotional, physical and spiritual dimension of grief and mourning, and frankly we were not only unprepared, we were ill-prepared for grief on this level.

Christians shouldn't grieve

The first myth to dispel is that Christians shouldn't grieve. Or, at least: 'Please don't grieve publicly where it can be seen and definitely don't grieve around me.'

I exaggerate! Or do I? My experience is that there is a subtle discomfort in many charismatic and evangelical churches around people who grieve. It doesn't fit with our victorious, triumphalist approach to the kingdom of God. I think, insidiously, the notion of grief has been sidelined. Not really embraced or welcomed and certainly something to 'move on' from. At the heart of this discomfort lies a well-known scripture written by Paul, 'But we do not want you to be uninformed, brothers, about those who are asleep, that you may not grieve as others do who have no hope.'[3]

Matthew McCulloch suggests:

> It's crucial, first of all, to accept that grief is not only unavoidable; it's also appropriate for Christians. When Paul says he doesn't want his

> friends to grieve as those who have no hope he doesn't say he doesn't want them to grieve. He's assuming grief. What matters to him is how they grieve. He wants them to grieve *with hope* and not without it.
>
> Sometimes with the best of intentions we Christians can fall into our own version of death rebranded as life. When a loved one dies, we say they're in a better place. We hold celebrations of life more often than funerals for the dead. And when we follow this route, sometimes we can even feel guilty for feeling so sad that our loved ones are gone. If they're with Jesus now, why can't I stop crying?
>
> Let me be clear: I do believe those who die in faith are in a better place. And of course, their lives are worth celebrating. But precisely because those loved ones are precious to us, they're worth crying over too.[4]

And my encouragement is this: nowhere in Scripture does it suggest that comfort ends grief or removes grief. It's important we get this, so that we can give ourselves and as a Church, to give others space to grieve, knowing they are safe with us. And more importantly maybe, just maybe, we can learn what it means to be a safe and comforting shoulder on which to lean.

So, for some, right now, this moment, while on this page in this chapter, know you have permission to mourn. You have permission to grieve. Your tears and your pain are validated. Every one of us at some stage in our lives will need to embrace this permission and this validation, and also be purveyors of this same permission and validation to others in our families and churches. And yes, there are different ways of handling different challenges, at different seasons on the journey. It's important to know there is no one right way and important that you and I do not get pressurised into any particular choices or patterns of behaviour; nor become complicit in pressuring others or giving off albeit vague vibrations of disapproval or discomfort.

Sometimes the truth of Scripture will help profoundly. But even here, there are surprises. Of course, I know the truth of Scripture that for me 'to live is Christ and to die is gain'.[5] I wrote the book on heaven, and people ask me was it cathartic. No, no and no again! Of course, I marvel at heaven and like Paul, I long to be there. That gives me rock-solid hope, it gives me great excitement at the thought of the upcoming adventure, and it gives me great joy for Joel, who is enjoying it. But that reality didn't help my grief; in fact, the process of writing added to the pain and generated even more tears.

Good grief is the grief that enables us to make the transition to a new phase of existence. Yes, the widow must learn to live alone; the parents must bear the bereft sense of loneliness brought on by the death of their son or daughter. Siblings must struggle as the often-forgotten mourners as they lose the love of their brother or sister.

It is a surprise for some to learn that sorrow and grief are to be expected and actually welcomed. If God is to heal the broken-hearted, then expect tears; if he is to heal the 'crushed in spirit', then expect tears.[6] Tears can either be a symptom or a sign of grief without hope, or they can reflect real, deep, even unimaginable loss and yet carry with them the hope and certainty both about the destination of our loved one and our own future healing.

Embracing pain is not negating faith. It's actually part of being in the likeness of God.[7] So yes, have hope, but don't deny your emotions. Pay attention to them. Feel what you feel and be free in expressing those feelings. Jesus certainly did.

'Jesus wept'

Grief that deals honestly with the pain is part of the healing process. Christ wept at the tomb of Lazarus, even though he was about to raise him from the dead. The Greek word *embrimaomai* used in this verse suggests Jesus was *deeply agitated and emotionally stirred*,[8] almost with groaning. He also agonised with loud crying and tears in Gethsemane at the thought of his own impending death.

So, this well-known scripture helps us and takes us to the death of one of Jesus' closest friends, Lazarus. This poignant moment actually produced the shortest verse in the Bible:

> When Jesus saw her weeping, and the Jews who had come along with her also weeping, he was deeply moved in his spirit and greatly troubled. And he said, 'Where have you laid him?' They said to him, 'Lord, come and see.' *Jesus wept.* So, the Jews said, 'See how he loved him!'[9]

Jesus had lost his own father sometime after the age of twelve; exactly when we are not sure. With all the positive statements we have made, Jesus does not minimise the pain of grief. He does not whitewash over it; he can share in it intimately. And in this short story with the shortest verse in the Bible, we get it. Jesus understands grief. He, more than anyone, knows that death is conquered, but it still leaves widows, orphans and bereaved parents behind. At the cross there is a remarkable exchange where he makes preparation, and says to Mary, 'Behold, your son!' and to John, 'Behold, your mother!'[10] Whatever else was being set up, Jesus understood the importance of close, trustworthy support at a time of grief.

In Matthew's Gospel, Jesus learns about the death of his beloved cousin John and the writer offers this glimpse:

'When Jesus heard what had happened, he withdrew by boat privately to a solitary place.'[11] Whatever else that tells us, it shows us that he knows and understands the need for privacy and a solitary place and experienced that need for himself.

In his narration of the same story, Bear Grylls describes it like this:

> From the moment I saw Yeshua that morning, I could tell something was wrong. We met him down by the lake, and he looked like he had the weight of the world on his shoulders. I'd never seen him so visibly upset . . . It took Yeshua a long time to recover from the death of his childhood friend and closest cousin. And in some ways, I don't think he ever got over it. If anything the death of Yohannan made Yeshua even more focussed on completing his mission.[12]

If you were to ask anyone who grieves the death of a loved one, one of the things they feel is that they grieve alone, that no one really understands them. One of our readers put it this way:

> I do believe no one really understands the depths of grief unless it happens to them. For others life just goes on whilst yours stops.

That is often true on a human level, but the liberating truth is that in our deepest pain, in those ceaseless seeping tears or in a tsunami of grief, Jesus has been there and understands it. He is described as a 'man of sorrows . . . acquainted with grief'.[13] To be acquainted with grief means to have personally experienced it, to know it firsthand, and to have a close, almost familiar understanding of its weight and reality. It implies a level of intimacy or familiarity with grief; not just having heard about it or seen it in others, but having lived through its pain yourself.

The psalmist talks about God storing our tears in a bottle.[14] It's good to pause and reflect on this. Putting it another way, not one tear is missed, not one tear goes unnoticed, not one tear is forgotten. Mourners sometimes collected their tears in small bottles and placed them in tombs as a sign of grief and love. David may have had that image in mind: *God Himself is the one collecting my tears.*

Our tears – all of them – from the single drop that is barely noticeable to the howls of pain and the moments of intense sobbing. Whether those tears are noticed by others or not, whether others can cope with our outbursts or distance themselves, Jesus validates your tears, metaphorically stores them, that's how important they are; he validates your pain, your burden. He doesn't rush it, trivialise it, or minimise it. Jesus wept; he validates it! We really do have a high priest who gets it, who empathises and who has been there.[15]

So it is, then, that my heart and goal in this chapter and in the ones that follow is to provide validation, understanding and permission. Before we can move into the promises of God, we need to know that every expression of grief is valid, and we need to know we have permission to grieve and mourn and that Scripture reveals and affirms both.

Types of grief and mourning in Scripture

There is a full list of metaphors from Scripture that follow the appendices. But let's explore together a handful of metaphors that were written by Jeremiah, the psalmists and Micah.

Jeremiah's list includes the following:

> See, LORD, how distressed I am! I am in torment within, and in my heart I am disturbed . . .
>
> My eyes fail from weeping, I am in torment within; my heart is poured out on the ground . . .
>
> He pierced my heart with arrows from his quiver.
>
> Oh, my anguish, my anguish! I writhe in pain. Oh, the agony of my heart! My heart pounds within me, I cannot keep silent.
>
> Pour out your heart like water in the presence of the Lord.[16]

The psalmist's list includes:

> Darkness is my closest friend.
>
> Be merciful to me, LORD, for I am in distress; my eyes grow weak with sorrow, my soul and body with grief. My life is consumed by anguish and my years by groaning . . .
>
> My heart is blighted and withered like grass; I forget to eat my food.
>
> The LORD is close to the broken-hearted and saves those who are crushed in spirit.
>
> I am worn out from my groaning. All night long I flood my bed with weeping and drench my couch with tears.
>
> cords of death . . . anguish of the grave . . .

Micah includes:

> Because of this I will weep and wail;
> I will go about barefoot and naked.
> I will howl like a jackal
> and moan like an owl.[17]

If I summarise these few scriptures, I think we get the picture that the Bible acknowledges the toll of grief and mourning with brutal honesty. Grief over death is pictured as a flood – unceasing, overwhelming, and deeply physical. Sorrow strikes the heart like a weapon. And it's crushing. Mourning is not silence; it is an anguished outpouring before the compassionate face of God. After loss, we may feel abandoned and wrapped in shadow. Scripture does not hide this truth.

Biblical grief is not restrained. It is often loud, physical, weeping, howling, groaning, shouting and openly expressed – whether as a personal cry to God or communal lament. These verses show God's people crying out in despair *to* God, not away from him.

Grief is 'somatic'; the body really does hold the score. Bereavement saps the body and soul. Grief includes physical collapse: exhaustion, failing sight, weakness of limbs. And it consumes our life, it really does take years. Grief causes wounding or internal damage as sharp as physical pain.

As we will explore in Chapter Nine, Jesus did say 'Blessed are those who mourn', but these words from Matthew are not a silver bullet, they are not a magic pill that somehow can be given to anybody who is grieving to expect daily, hourly comfort in some kind of calibrated way. This blessing, real as it is, does not take away grief.

Each heart knows its own grief

In Proverbs 14:10 (translations vary a bit[18]) the text is in effect saying, 'Each heart knows its own grief'. It was after an *All About Heaven* event in Vancouver that the church leaders, Steven and Shinnie Abraham, reminded Gill and me of this verse.

Similarly, Proverbs describes: 'Death and Destruction lie open before the Lord – how much more do human hearts!'[19] and in 1 Kings we read: 'You alone know every human heart'.[20] Behind these scriptures lies a very simple truth; we can't put one approach, one scripture, one church response, one guarantee, or one set of behaviours or experiences on different individuals. It really can't work like that.

Remember the quote a few paragraphs back? 'I do believe no one really understands the depths of grief unless it happens to them. For others life just goes on whilst yours stops.'

No one other than Jesus himself can ever really know what the grief of another is truly like. Let me share how some of my friends describe this:

> Three years after being widowed, I continually remind married friends that someday this will happen to one of them. I tell them you aren't going to understand till it happens how it will be. They don't get it. But they know I'm here for them. I'll just sit with them, hold them, talk if they want to, sit quiet if they don't. I have seen all sorts of reactions from friends.

Every journey of sorrow has its own unique map. As we shall see God's intent is for hearts to heal but he has his own unique way and his own unique timetable for each person. That's why it's important we each need to know our grief is valid and we have permission to mourn and equally we should never presume to know how others should deal with their pain.

Kessler says: 'There is no one right way to do grief. You know, there's no map for grief. Grief is organic. You do it your way.'[21]

There's no right way to grieve, just different ways, and I think that's helpful and true. Roger Greene says, 'The way a person grieves and mourns a death is unique to them. We should not compare ourselves and think we are failing in some way if we aren't grieving as society expects.'[22]

People survive in different ways; some people survive and find it helpful to talk, others cannot handle words or sound, they need silence. Some need hugs, some need long walks in solitude. Everyone who grieves deals with unimaginable pain in their own way, and everyone has permission to do that, and can likely find in Scripture a reflection of others who have walked a similar path in a similar way. And everyone is entitled to do that without judgement.

How does this manifest in practical ways? In the next chapter we take a look a grief in practice.

Chapter Four

Grief in Practice

With permission and validation breathed into us from the Scriptures, it doesn't mean it's a comfortable or desirable journey we find ourselves on. Someone once described it as 'a ticket we never asked for, for a journey we never wanted'.[1]

Five stages or a journey?

If you're already familiar with the so-called stages of grief you have psychiatrist Elisabeth Kübler-Ross to thank for it.[2] She pioneered early thinking and understanding on grief, conducting interviews with more than 200 terminally ill patients. Originally this research was not about those left behind, but for those who were dying. However, her notion that there are five stages of grief has been widely adopted by many grief counsellors.

At first glance, these stages can appear helpful and indeed, for some they can be. However, as we saw earlier,

'Each heart knows its own grief', and for some, while they may indeed go through grief in a linear pattern, others do not. In recent years, critics have argued that the model can oversimplify grief and create unrealistic expectations.

David Kessler in particular clarified that grief is non-linear and highly individual. Notes on his comments and several new models of grief have subsequently been proposed and there is a resource available as a PDF at the end of this book.

For most of us, grief is a journey which does not fit into neatly tightly defined boxes or stages but is rather a roller coaster of emotions that does not proceed in an orderly or predictable pattern. And as we shall see in Chapter Nine, the Word of God and the comfort of the Holy Spirit can profoundly impact the nature, the stages and the timing of our journey.

Practical descriptions of grief

One of the commonly asked questions is, 'What's the difference between grieving and mourning?' David Kessler explains, 'Grief is what's going on inside of us while mourning is what we do on the outside'.[3] He goes on to say 'that while everyone grieves differently, we all have in common the need for our grief to be witnessed'.[4]

Grief at times disables you. You can still do things, but your abilities are not what they were. For Gill and me, we calibrate our mental acuity as running at around 70 per cent of normal; our physical and emotional strength and well-being probably less than 70 per cent. That's the reality of grief. One of the strange outcomes of grief I've noticed is preoccupation in the mind. You find yourself somewhere else, doing something else, thinking of someone else. It was brought home to me as I was given a glass of water to take some vitamins over breakfast. Gill gave it to me; I held out my hand, but my mind was back with Joel in some hospital setting. My mouth was speaking to Gill, but my mind was not remotely engaging in any way. It was not intentionally rude, it was just my mind was engaged somewhere else without choosing it. I found especially in the early months and years that my mind would take itself off somewhere else so much of the time, and it's so hard to get it focused where it should be. I came to see it like one of those rubber bungees that you see used in fairgrounds, or certain kinds of sports training exercises. You run against that bungie but as soon as you stop running, the thing pulls you back and you have no choice.

I spilled the water and Gill said I blamed her. I was sorry! In reality I spoke a disconnected response with my mouth while my head was somewhere else. And of course, it's hard for your spouse, for your partner or for those around you, because you say things that are not hurtful in intent or even hurtful in your head; but because your brain is somewhere else with something else going on, unintended words come out garbled and sometimes they are damaging. Grief has a nasty habit of leaving you discombobulated.

I still have a rainbow of emotions. I still do have red, blue, indigo, but now there's a band of black that was not there before – part of my life is coloured black now. And that's not lack of faith or hope, it's honesty; it doesn't need healing, it's part of the forming process of God in me.

Grief is like a looming shadow, lurking hidden in the mist of every day. And she can present her fullest, darkest shape, emerging out of the mist into close proximity when you don't expect it and when you don't want it. Grief doesn't go away. I was chatting to one psychiatrist friend who described it this way: 'You can hide from grief, busy it away, suppress it, ignore it or run from it; but grief bides its time hidden away and when it chooses, it finds its way out.'

Or as I wrote in an attempt to process my own journey in the moment; 'Every now and then, without warning or alert, a sharp shard of grief pierces the day uninvited, and take's the soul's breath away' and then as I took notice of the beautiful nature I was surrounded by at the same moment, 'Today's small moment of grief, and today's raw soul, had heaven's paintbrush to colour wash away the grey; and fill that painful space with healing colour, scent and form.'

What others say

Having explored descriptions and metaphors in Scripture, it can leave us affirmed and confident that we have 'permission' to grieve and mourn. Seeing how others experience grief and express their mourning can be reassuring and also empowering. Seeing the range of emotions that others describe can reassure you and me that we are normal, we are not going mad, we are not unspiritual, and others have been there too!

I asked readers of the book *All About Heaven* to share their own way of viewing grief and mourning. To give you some examples, here is just a handful from the responses:[5]

> There is nothing anyone can say. Words mean nothing even though I am using a lot of them. No one, however well-meaning, can ever put a verbal band aid on grief.
>
> Grief and love are woven together. Our grief is only so intense because of how intense the love was.
>
> Grief is like bouncing along on the bottom of a dark tunnel; every now and then you will get a glimmer of light which will go out again and another time the glimmer of light will stay for a little bit longer. It will come and go over a period, then one day you will realise that half an hour has gone by without thinking about Joel.

It felt like a dark, dark tunnel with no visible end.

In my darkest days, days where the pain was so savage I couldn't hardly breathe at points . . . physical pain like long shards of hot glass pushed up into the abdomen.

Some days I wanted to scream out loud in pain and several days I did just that.

What struck me in the early days of being a young widow . . . it felt as though an earthquake had occurred. The ground didn't just tremble, it shifted from under me in one gaping chasm. My world had dissolved and with it, my surety of foot, my confidence and trust and with it, my reason for being.

I felt truly untethered, left afloat like a fragile balloon that has been suddenly set loose from its thread that had connected it to base. Left with no way of controlling the elements around itself and the direction of travel. At the mercy of all, vulnerable, all sense of security gone.

All that was left and that I could hold on to, were the very thoughts held in my head and my spiritual beliefs and these too were now under severe challenge. It was the deepest, blackest, loneliest place of despair. It didn't feel like a tunnel that I could slowly navigate, but a sharp-sided pit with no way out except perhaps by way of a giant enormous hand to stretch down and pull me free of it.

I think to be honest his death was so unexpected that I went into a numbness and when I think of him now, I think that numbness is still there.

The unpredictability of tears has been hard. I could – and still can – be fine one minute and lost in tissues the next. Wham! No warning. Some days fine but others . . . tears have no sense of courtesy! They just butt in!

I felt like people wanted me to be better but didn't know how to make me better. People didn't want to talk about it, or about my husband, and they don't want me to talk about him.

I was desperate to get through the first five years. I just had to sit in the sadness and somehow, in that place, the sadness was the space in which I got through those five years.

I've known both parents pass away, a brother too, the loss of ministry opportunities and what I believed to be a life calling. Grief can cause an isolation where no one else knows or understands what you are experiencing at any one stage. Life may go on as normal for all around you, but you are faced with the ongoing, seemingly never-ending cavern of life, unexplained dashed hopes, and an emptiness that nothing and no one can seemingly fill.

As a widow it's different to being a parent or a son or daughter. There is loss of course for each of us but for a widow there's a change in relationship and perceived status that is different for parents and children. I am now single again; If I don't remarry I can feel 'judged' for not moving on. If I do remarry, I feel judged for forgetting him!

'The person you thought you were may seem changed, erratic, forgetful, helpless, dull or out of control, changed in many ways; all these are normal signs of grief. You will move through them as you journey through grief, you will never be quite the same again the journey will not last forever you will emerge in a way that will be right for you. You may even feel angry even furious outraged this is normal and healthy. Talk about your anger and express it in non-hurtful ways. Kick or punch a mattress or pillow find a place where you can scream without upsetting others maybe a railway track and scream as the train comes near. You may feel very very sad. Life may seem to have lost all meaning these feelings are temporary too and will pass. You may fear what's ahead you already know the loneliness and the darkness expect the ride to be full of ups and downs like a rollercoaster. Know that after each down comes an up. The pits will become less deep and dark. Understand that you must journey through your grief. Grief is a journey you've been given the ticket for. The journey and the ticket which you didn't ask for, didn't deserve and most definitely didn't want. Your grief is unique to you, no one can feel it just as you do. But there are others who have known similar pain and remember the journey will not last forever.'[6]

> At times the pain of grief felt like a gnawing homesickness for the place where I used to live and missed so much . . . The emotional ground beneath my feet had shifted so much that nothing was as it had been. There was no familiar ground even in familiar places. It was like living abroad – even when walking down familiar streets and seeing familiar faces.[7]

One friend, Glenys Hart, articulated it like this:

> I think I felt a bit like Alice who fell down a deep dark hole. To me the sides all closed in and

looking up there was no sunlight and I couldn't imagine ever being able to climb up and get out of the hole. After a while I also felt like I had drunk the contents of the bottle like Alice, and become so small and insignificant that people didn't notice me anymore. I so desperately wanted to be back in the sunlight so living in that dark night of the soul for so long was perhaps the hardest thing that I had ever experienced – long and interminable!

I felt other people who hadn't experienced grief were uncomfortable around me and conveyed their feelings that I should be over it all, which brought condemnation on top of the grief. There were others who just didn't know what to say, so they avoided me which I guess was what made me feel like I had shrunk and was so small they didn't see me.

There is no handbook or promised timeframe or signpost to say just 100 metres more to travel, or another two weeks, or this time next year, you will be in a different place. The sat nav for any modern-day direction of travel is replaced by a signal-less guessing of which way to turn and what to do. Life is on hold. The joy and relief of returning strength is so precious. A shaft of light is so gratefully received.

For Gill and me, circumstances, speed and brutality took us through a deeply traumatic and shocking experience. And it's little surprise, then, what that turbulence can do to the mind and its need to process, resolve and heal over time. I had some days even two to three years later where a tsunami of grief would catch me out, it would erupt, and I would find myself screaming out loud with the pain. For Gill it has been years of 'flashbacks' at night. Every single night for a long time she was back in the hospital, reliving some of the conversations, and the brutal treatments given to Joel that ended up being futile.

We prayed together and it would ease some. We had intercessors pray and the church pray and again it would ease up.

There are moments that have come out of the blue that have stopped me in my tracks and taken all the breath from my lungs. Sometimes an unstoppable scream or howl of pain explodes when the reality of Joel's departure or the mountain-size feeling of deep sorrow makes me crumble to the floor or bend over double with the pain.

All that and more are the everyday realities of those who grieve.

Grief and church

Going to church is something many, probably most, people struggle with and it's totally understandable. Everyone else is joyful and/or victorious; and it seems to trivialise pain and suffering and can be so unhelpful. People handle this differently; however, I would say categorically, do not be under pressure to rush back. You may well find an ebb and flow or a rhythm that works for you. There may be smaller groups in the church that could offer a point of love, prayer and connection, or you may find that concept even more troubling than attending on Sundays!

One friend described it this way:

> I walked through the darkest time of my life, probably into depression, although that was never officially diagnosed. I found that I couldn't go to church, which I had always loved. Many Sundays, my husband would say to me: 'Why don't you try?' I would get dressed, walk to the car, but be almost physically unable to even get in the car, or if I did, I would get to the church and be unable to go in. I couldn't worship the God that I had known and loved for years. I used to say to him, 'I can never stop believing in you, because I have seen you do too much, but I don't think I like you anymore and I don't think I want to walk with you anymore!' Some people were shocked,

> but it is good to be honest with God and it wasn't rebellious, it was the truth and now I'm sure that God understood.[8]

Another friend wrote:

> Sunday I tried to go to church. I didn't last more than five minutes before leaving again. It was all joyful singing. The feeling of not being on the same planet as the others. It was almost an insult to my suffering. Other people's lives go on, and yours is shattered into a thousand pieces.[9]

For the first year or so Gill and I found it difficult to go to church gatherings. There were lots of reasons for that, but one of the most obvious was that the pain of trying to make conversation before or after the gathering was unhelpful, and too acute for us to bear. I unpack this a little later in the book but we made sure we entered a few minutes late, sat by the exit and left before the last song or prayer completed.

I'll never forget one of the early *All About Heaven* evening events we presented. At the end there was a line of folk who wanted to talk and/or receive some prayer. One couple stood with the church leaders talking and praying for nearly an hour. That day was the first day in more than a year that they could physically and emotionally cope with going back to church since their young child had died unexpectedly in her sleep. It's OK if that is your experience too.

Another friend wrote:

> After my wife died, I initially stayed with my local church, but attendance quickly became spasmodic until it stopped altogether. Although I experienced love and support from some of the people who I knew there, it was difficult to see everyone else carrying on as normal. The worst times were when we were asked during the service to greet someone, with the implication that we would be cheerful while doing so. The after-service coffee time was also challenging. Standing on your own watching everyone else chatting as couples (or at least that's what it seemed like) is soul-destroying. Then, the slow walk or drive home to an empty house and spending the rest of the day on your own. I understand now why for some single people Sunday can be the worst day of the week.[10]

Close friends of ours Steve and Lorraine Thomas have been in international pastoral ministry for decades. Their experience is a comfort into which we have leaned several times in our lives. One couple that Steve and Lorraine knew well thought they were backsliding when they couldn't go to church. Their (grown) child had died from cancer at the age of thirty-six. Steve and Lorraine spent nine months with them, one session a month praying, allowing them to have a voice for their story; finding out how they were feeling, finding out how they were getting on. Asking the questions, 'What's going on in your heart and mind?' Then reassuring this couple, making it clear they were not backsliding. Making it clear it was OK not to praise God from day one. Making it clear you didn't have to be attending church on some kind of grief spirituality time chart.

One of our challenges was the singing of songs. Gill came back from a craft evening and told me that one of her friends had said to her, 'So glad you weren't there last Sunday.' When pressed, she expanded, 'Nearly all the songs were about heaven and the grave and death.' This friend understood something, and in her love for Gill reflected her understanding. For the first few months after Joel died, every Sunday gathering we attended, there were songs about death and heaven. Every Sunday.

And it's painful. Not because I disagree with the theology, but because the singing and the words themselves touch memories, touch the wellspring of grief still ready and waiting to pour out its tears. And mostly I can't sing. Not because I lack faith in the concept but because the painful reality of Joel's dying comes flooding back into my mind like a 3D IMAX and I'm back there with him. Gill's friend instinctively understood that and wanted to protect Gill.

Proverbs understands the impact of songs on the bereaved and gives us a practical insight: 'Singing cheerful songs to a person with a heavy heart is like taking someone's coat in cold weather or pouring vinegar in a wound.'[11]

In Chapter Ten we see how finding God in the midst of grief is possible and discover that at some point on the journey, church attendance becomes possible, even desirable again. But giving those who struggle the time and process they need without judgement, or without communicating disappointment or disapproval is a good, helpful and godly thing to do.

Grief and the marriage myth

It is very true that marriages go through significant stress when a child dies, and it is commonly quoted that 80 per cent of marriages experiencing child loss will end in divorce. It is, however, a social media myth. The reality is that break-up rates are the same.[12] In one of the most recently available reviews, it highlights that losing a child can put immense strain on a marriage – leading to communication breakdown, emotional distance and conflict, and yet the same review shows some couples grow closer.[13]

One of the many reasons for these marriage stressors is the very different way couples grieve and the impact of each on their spouse. Gill and I, in common with most couples, grieve differently. I tend towards inward thinking, and I don't much want sound or conversation. Gill thrives better on appropriate conversation, and in order to prevent her mind going to painful places, she likes to have TV, YouTube or something else playing.

And of course, practically, these polar opposite tendencies are inevitably going to produce tensions. Understanding it is not abnormal, is a help in itself, and then importantly finding ways to dialogue it through, making room for each other's needs.

Living grief

There are situations where grief is an ongoing, unresolved continuum. What I mean by that is the person you love is going through a protracted illness and each day or each week you are losing more. The obvious scenarios include illnesses like dementia, long-term cancers, MS, muscular dystrophy, motor neurone disease, hospice; the list is long.

For five years our friend Lorraine was in a situation with parents who had dementia. It was a different kind of grief, and it was real grief, because they were no longer who they once were. When they died, she said, 'I felt robbed. It didn't hit as hard as it might have when it happened because they were already lost to me in some way.'

This type of grief has additional challenges. In our case with Joel, we had a cocktail of multiple shocks, grief and pain all condensed into a short timeframe that caught us unaware and left us reeling. It was the case a few times that the next shock or trauma was unleashed before we had even begun to process the preceding shock or trauma. We had fresh waves of grief every day as we saw brutal treatments, observed steady decline and faced each day with shockingly sharp shards of glass causing our souls and sometimes our voices to cry out. But alongside all that was the relentless, almost unbearable, additional grief of knowing the future would never be the same and dreading the icy darkness that this new future would one day bring.

Finding God on this journey and making sure you have practical and caring support is essential for handling the journey well.

Grief at large

This book is intentionally focused on grief from loss and death because that is our journey. However, it is important to say there are multiple ranges of reactions to grief and a whole variety of ways in which people do mourn. These can also include types of grief not related to death. So, for example, grief of infertility, divorce, job loss, multiple miscarriages, multiple redundancies and even long-term depression. I have worked with individuals and married couples who have been through the grief of a lost business and shattered dreams. The loss of pets can also be deeply distressing for many.

So, while the degree of grief and mourning is likely and substantially different, it is still grief and knowing that there is permission to grieve and knowing that there are the promises of God to lean into can be a real healing insight.

Prolonged grief

It is important to be aware of what is known as complicated grief or prolonged grief disorder. This is grief that doesn't subside. And the normal grief response which allows moving forward over time is not present: 'Complicated grief, also known as prolonged grief disorder, is grief that doesn't seem to get better. This form of grief prevents healing and affects your ability to resume daily life. Research suggests that about 7% to 10% of bereaved adults experience this type of grief.'[14]

I can only mention this in passing as I am not competent or qualified to address it. It's a specialist area of counselling. However, it is also super important that I do flag it, because it may be, as you read this, you recognise this in yourself or someone you care for, and seeking appropriate help is critical. If you feel like your grief is permanently disabling, then this is the most likely reason.

Resources and sources of support appear at the end of the book.

Chapter Five

Anniversaries

It's no surprise that anniversaries can be some of the hardest moments for those who are grieving. Christmas, birthdays, weddings, anniversaries and especially the date of the loss itself – they all carry emotional weight that can catch us off guard. These are moments that seem designed to remind us of who is missing, whether we want the reminder or not.

These days are milestones which act as uninvited, unwelcome reminders. In normal life, milestones calibrate distance as hard facts. For us they measure the distance back to the death of our loved one and with their stark reminder, our grief is reopened.

Sometimes the experience can be almost crushingly overwhelming. Some days hit hard. Others pass more quietly than we expected. In fact, the build-up to the day can be worse than the day itself. And when the day feels less painful than we thought, we can even end up feeling guilty 'This day should be really hard, am I already forgetting my loved one?' These thoughts are common, and they don't mean you've forgotten. They just remind us that grief isn't predictable.

The truth is that you or I can never know for sure what the day will bring and this uncertainty can add to the challenge. Will the day be this or that, one or the other? And that too can add to the turbulence. What is clear to all is that the absence shouts louder on special days. Birthdays, Christmas, wedding anniversaries, the absence of our loved one is shoved in our face. Days and traditions that once brought great joy can now feel like a hot knife cutting into tender souls; or like a laser surgically applied to old wounds, partly healed but now reopened.

Unsurprisingly, many of us struggle with whether to continue old traditions, adapt them or create new ones. That struggle can compound with differing family members and differing preferences. What might appeal deeply to me might be a nightmare for Gill or another member of the family. That needs careful navigation with tender conversations as we try to find space to honour each person's preferences.

No right way

There is no right or wrong way. Some visit graves, light candles, gather with others; some prefer to be alone and reflect quietly. Some smile through tears; others simply cry. Often on these days there's a mixture that can include sadness, gratitude, nostalgia. Grief doesn't follow a script. It's OK to do none or all of these things. For those who are able, it's wise to think ahead, especially for the first few years. Perhaps have a conversation with each family member and chat through their feelings or expectations. Especially check out what you might be thinking of posting online; some really don't want social media posting on anniversaries.

Our first anniversary

The 20 December 2019 at 12.57 was the first anniversary of Joel's death.

Waiting for the day was like the long weeks waiting for the funeral. Knowing you couldn't change the date, knowing you must face it and yet longing for it all to be over.

Every year the family faces this day with apprehension. It's the anniversary no one wants, and everyone dreads; and of course, we each handle every year very differently.

On this first year, we chose to go out walking with some caring friends in Winchester, a beautiful city not far from our home. To begin with, the weather was great, but as we approached the hour it began to pour with rain. We thought we had left plenty of time and yet as it turned out we ended up strangely pressed for time. I kept looking at my watch every ten minutes or so, checking and dreading the 12.57 moment.

Excusing ourselves from our friends, Gill and I, arm in arm, walked at a pace, trying to get to Winchester Cathedral by 12.56. We had wanted to gather our thoughts and reflect in the cathedral itself. In the end, time ran out in an abrupt manner. We literally stopped, arms around each other, weeping together as the minute hand marked our moment, his final moment. We were under an archway of trees, tears and rain streaming down our faces, turning our heads away from oncoming hordes of people. This was an intensely private moment, an intimate moment; a grief embrace, as best we could in the middle of hordes of oblivious happy shoppers following their Christmas instincts while we wept out our 12.57 pain to no one in particular.

Shortly afterwards, we found a small chapel nearby. We went in there alone and wept again. I'll never forget the shock as Gill cried out aloud in the silent chapel, 'Oh the pain, will it ever get better?' It was a pain-seared day and it is etched in my memory.

At these times, we are on an unchosen journey of grief through an unchosen topography, the valley of 'deepest darkness'.[1] Like a long journey on UK roads when you get unexpected, deeply impacting gridlock, everything grinds to a halt, there's no way back and seemingly no way forwards and then grief permeates: heart, eyes, breathing and deep, deep in the soul.

We had a range of thoughts and emotions around this day. At the beginning of the day, Gill was thinking about

Mary and the angels speaking and she woke up thinking about the scripture, 'Why do you look for the living among the dead?'[2]

Gill said to me, 'If we are believing in heaven and resurrection and believing that Joel is alive somewhere wonderful, doing something wonderful, we don't really want to focus on that last day and be reminded of the sorrow. Instead, we should be looking back and celebrating the fact that this is the anniversary of a whole year in heaven.'

So yes! This was the first anniversary. And yes, we had a year of grief, a year walking in the valley of 'deepest darkness'. However, Joel has not had a year of grief, he has had a year of adventure, and today marked the anniversary of his first day in paradise; his first day of safety, joy, health and purpose in the arms of Jesus.

In the middle of the sorrow and painful memories, we found ourselves wondering what he had been doing for a whole year in heaven; and smiling at the thought of him sharing that with us when we did finally meet up.

Joel David Oliver really is home free, and in the bittersweet mix of it all, somehow we wanted to celebrate his gain rather than only focusing on mourning our loss.

Wedding anniversaries

For some, the anniversary is a reminder of the direct loss of your life's partner. One friend, wrote this:

> Today is our wedding anniversary and sixty-four years is a big hole to fill – silly little things are big things, like I always made two cups of coffee before we prayed at 10.30 and on our anniversary, I only put out one cup and it hurt bad.[3]

For others, you're 'celebrating' a wedding anniversary with the loss of a son or daughter or sibling. Anniversaries are often triggers for moments of grief and reminders of loss. Gill and I were dreading our first wedding anniversary after Joel died. Joel had always been creative and generous-hearted.

That first anniversary we were to experience a totally unexpected touch from heaven which is unpacked in Chapter Nine. But this was a day with turbulently conflicting emotions. In essence, a hazy mix of both gratitude and unwanted heavy weight. Gratitude for the years we had together but the unavoidable inescapable impenetrable weight of knowing the deepest loss any parent can bear.

> Child loss doesn't just impact the heart of a parent. It deeply affects marriage. Grief is raw and unpredictable, and when two people grieve differently, it can feel like you are worlds apart under the same roof. One of might need to talk, while the other goes silent. One might cry, while the other holds it all in. When emotions run

> this deep, it's easy to mistake our partner's way of grieving as distance – or worse, as not caring. The truth is, we're both trying to survive the unthinkable in the only way we know how.[4]

If Gill and I have learned anything after forty-nine years of marriage, it is that grief has changed us and changed our relationship, but we have weathered the multiple storms and hurricane-strength winds; we can say with God's help we have learned to give each other permission and encouragement to grieve differently.

Christmas

Amid the air of cheer and festive spirit that graces the Christmas holiday season, those who grieve bear the heavy burden of loss. Each toast, each meal, each smile and each gift is a reminder of who is missing from these moments. Grievers have the exhausting role of finding joy through the pain at a time when reminders are everywhere.

Many readers will have spent weeks, maybe months, preparing for the biggest annual family get-together. For most, the plans and the shared meals, the exchange of gifts and the enjoyment of shared family traditions bring a sense of joyful anticipation and grateful participation.

But for some, the approach of Christmas is like a looming precipice, a weary traveller already on an unchosen journey in the valley of 'deepest darkness', seeing even deeper darkness ahead. And yes, especially in the early years for many readers, their friends, their family, or their neighbours, that is the journey.

One memory surfaces with painful clarity. Gill is a lover of all things Christmas. Snow, manger scenes, children singing carols and mince pies. On the first Christmas after Joel's death, she was in a town on her own, returning some unused medications to a pharmacy. Close by, the Salvation Army was playing carols. Normally this would have produced a moment of joy, seasonal reflection and happy conversations with other listeners. This experience, however, became a brutal moment. Great pain pushed its way to the surface like some unwelcome volcanic activity; inevitable, maybe, and unstoppable, definitely. The overriding response was, 'How could they be playing?' It was an intrusion; she wanted to cry out, 'Stop playing and go away!'

Some sensitive churches offer what have come to be called 'Blue Christmas' or 'Longest Night' services around the Christmas season. These services are quieter and more reflective than traditional Christmas celebrations, offering space for people who are grieving or hurting. They often include candle lighting, prayers and words of comfort, reminding participants that Christ came as light in the darkness.

Support and acknowledgement matter

A simple message, a shared memory, or just being there for someone can mean everything. Grief can feel isolating and knowing that others remember can be deeply comforting. For those who look on, finding some way to reach out can be difficult, even risky; but for those who grieve, it can be especially meaningful. This is true of words and actions.

Friends of ours offered to be with us on the first anniversary. Recalling their thinking process, they remembered approaching it with uncertainty, even a sense of impotence, but with great love and concern for us. They found themselves wanting to be thoughtful, wanting to care and wanting to be present, and yet at the same time without a clue as to what would really help.

They found the words to express their love and care for us. They told us they didn't want us to be on our own unless that's what we wanted. They made it clear the choices were ours and doing nothing was fine. They offered suggestions of their own, which included spending some moments together reflecting and praying. Having lunch together. Walking together. We were so raw and fragile with the pain of it all, it was a risk for them, but the outcome was the best that could have been achieved for us.

Finding words for others

Grief is not linear, it is cyclical. Time does not erase grief; it reshapes it. Anniversaries often bring back memories and emotions with a surprising intensity. A person might feel they have 'moved forwards a bit', only to find themselves deeply affected when a significant date arrives. For that reason, the thought and care of others is deeply meaningful.

An email or a card with thoughtful words reminds the grieving friend that you have carved out time in your busy world, overcome your own hurdle of doubt and worry of getting it wrong and you have done your best to add comfort and strength to show you care.

Words that worked

Our next two chapters deal with both helpful and unhelpful responses. Here are two examples of words that meant a great deal to us on that first anniversary of Joel's death:

> Dear Dave and Gill, Just to let you know we are standing with you in prayer today, the anniversary of Joel's death. Knowing you will be reliving his last days I'm sure the pain will be even more acute. Praying for strength, grace and his comfort. We continue to pray for you all.

> Dear Dave and Gill, Just to say we are thinking of you both and the whole family today. Remembering you in prayer. Trusting you and the family experience his grace over the next few days. Much love . . .[5]

These emails and many others like them brought healing tears. Yes, most were short and yes, most helped remind us in our pain that we were not on our own.

One friend had the courage to write a poem to us which was especially meaningful:

Father Mother's Son who Died

TINY things ridicule death with hope to
dismantle our fears.
From dark black buried places, Life!
After cold snowy winters, returning clumped primroses,
velvet violets, yellow daffodils,
and when winters ice has flown,
snowdrops!
Last year birds flew far away, but look you now,
swallows returning across skies of blue!

Anthony L. Kelton

Anniversaries and time

Grief changes over time, but whether anniversaries get 'easier' is a deeply personal experience. Some people find that as the years pass, the intensity of grief softens, and anniversaries become moments of reflection rather than overwhelming sorrow. Others continue to feel deep pain on those dates, even decades later.

Here are a few observations about grief and anniversaries over time:

The initial pain lessens, but the love remains. In the early years, grief on anniversaries can feel unbearable, but with time, the rawness fades. You don't forget or stop missing the person, but the pain becomes more manageable.

For some, *anniversaries can shift from pain to meaning.* Initially, anniversaries will likely bring a wave of fresh and intense grief, but over time, they can become opportunities for remembrance, gratitude, or even celebration of the person's life rather than just their passing. New traditions may emerge; you may find yourself initiating things to plan ahead for that day.

However, even with all that said as intimated grief is not linear, nor does healing follow a straight line. Some years, an anniversary might feel easier, while another year, a memory or life event can stir up emotions again.

New life chapters change the perspective. As time passes, new relationships, experiences and personal growth can influence how you relate to your grief. You may find new ways to honour or remember your loved one, or their absence may integrate into your life differently.

Triggers can still surprise you. Even years later, a song, a scent, or a place might suddenly bring back a strong wave of emotion. I have one friend who associates the death of his mum with a perfume. Strong scents can trigger memories and grief responses. For me, occasionally on my boat touching Joel's fishing gear can stop me like hitting an invisible forcefield and I can still gasp with shock and pain. Other times I can put a lure on the line and find pleasure and gratitude as I cast the line into the water.

This kind of response is normal and doesn't mean you or I are 'going backwards' – it's just part of the lifelong unpredictability that goes with the turf.

New responses. Many find comfort in keeping a sense of connection – through traditions, or intentionally talking about their loved ones. Others might decide on acts of kindness, charitable giving in the name of their loved one. This can turn anniversary grief into something meaningful, hopeful, positive and something that makes a difference to others. Others I have watched have started an annual event, maybe a run, using social media to stir up interest and participation and using the anniversary to make a difference to some cause special to them and the memory of their loved one.

However each anniversary impacts you, let's remind ourselves there is no right or wrong way to grieve, and no right or wrong way to handle different types of anniversary. Let's also remind ourselves that like the tide, there can be an ebb and flow. Dependent on the tide on that day, your grief may seem a distant horizon or like it's all the way 'out'. And at other times it can feel like its high tide all the way up in your face and to the very edges of your soul.

Chapter Six

Help That Hurts

One of the many surprises for our family was the inability of church friends in conversations, emails or texts to find words that helped. In fact, I guesstimated it as roughly fifty/fifty whether something someone said was likely to be helpful or unhelpful. And particularly during Joel's hospitalisation with the traumatic events, some of those well-meaning communications left me reeling with more pain than I began with. And what's worse still, is that in most cases those folk will never know.

C.S. Lewis understood this so well and I remember the relief when reading his comments in *A Grief Observed* where he says: 'I see people, as they approach me, trying to make up their minds whether they'll "say something about it" or not. I hate if they do, and if they don't.'[1]

I was relieved, because countless times I have experienced that sensation, that lump of concrete in the pit of my stomach as I approach a bereaved person or family, crying to God, 'Please give me some words.' It's hard, and we often don't know what to say. And like most of us, I suspect, with the best of intentions, I have gone ahead and made the grieving friend or church member feel worse after our encounter and not better.

I'm not judging here, either. I think there are several reasons why it's so hard to find the right words or to make the right approach to those who have been bereaved. In this chapter I hope to share the main reasons why it is so difficult and offer some examples. And it may surprise you that my conclusion is that church members have particular challenges that non-Christians are not afflicted with. As a result, there is a certain inevitability that Christians will find it hard.

This chapter will attempt to illustrate some specific examples of well-meaning words that have brought damage!

The need for victory in church

Gill and I have run thirty or more *All About Heaven* evening events. At nearly every event we have had people coming to talk to us (roughly 10 per cent of every audience) who would share their pain in grief, and commonly share the inability of their church community to understand and help them through it. Many, probably the majority, of those we spoke to had never been able to truly share their grief with their church leaders or church family. Even though we understood this from our own journey, it was still surprising to see the scale.

Church leaders trying to fix grief

One of the most common responses we picked up was church leaders and/or church family members who were trying to 'fix grief', trying to get people to 'move on' from grief. Church families who were unwittingly communicating the notion that grief was somehow not triumphant, not victorious and not really acceptable. Somehow those who were grieving instinctively knew that this was dangerous territory, and out of self-protection kept themselves from it.

Charismatic churches, house church and to some degree the evangelical movement is essentially a young movement with a victorious eschatology. The expansive teaching on the kingdom of God, welcome as it was, and still is, has, however, left us with a sanitisation of grief.

This means there can be an unwitting discomfort in church circles with anybody who's not overtly victorious following the death of a loved one. We know the scripture 'so that you do not grieve like the rest of mankind, who have no hope'[2]. The problem is, a victorious-minded church focuses on the hope and wants those of us who have suffered loss to only exhibit hope. It's almost as if unwittingly the Church only has room for hope and no room for grief. Of course, that's never the overt intention, but nonetheless how cruel, how ungodly. Added to which there's a hidden disappointment, embarrassment or shame in prayers for healing that did not get answered with healing.

Please be real with yourself, your faith and your church. There are exceptions but, in my experience, I have seen very few people with genuinely terminal illnesses get healed. Can I repeat that, so you don't miss it? Please! I have prayed for the sick over forty years as a church leader and again, from my perspective, in the main, people prayed for with genuinely terminal illnesses did not get healed. Death is not defeat, it's a promise, it's a certainty, a God-bounded inevitable outcome that on one level should not shock or surprise us. It should not rock our faith and most definitely it should not make us clumsy in mourning 'with those who mourn' (Romans 12:15).

Of all people on earth, those of us in the family of God should be the best at mourning 'with those who mourn' and yet often it seems the reverse is true. Reflecting upon this, I found myself thinking about the huge emphasis on prayer and healing, good as that is, in our Bible teaching and small-group life. And even though the reality is that every church member will at some point face death and dying, how much time and teaching and exposure is given to handling death, dying and grief?

And I suppose inevitably there's the process that follows a pattern: we prayed for the healing, it hasn't happened; so, our instinct is, we must be spiritual so let's at least be victorious in death! That's one of the unhelpful pressures, to try to fix it for people, to try to fix the awkward moments, to try to suppress the apparent lack of victory.

Examples of the unhelpful

I could give you many examples. I was on a telephone call and at significant personal cost I had vulnerably shared some grief. And in an unexpected outburst, I let out a howl of deep anguish that caught me by surprise. I heard the person I was speaking to comment that this sounded demonic. I understand the unnerving impact of an unexpected howl, but it was grief at its most intense vulnerably shared and certainly not demonic!

Another individual, maybe wondering if I was still serving God fully, told me the story of a friend who had stood on his wife's grave and declared that he would serve the kingdom. The unspoken inference being, 'David, you need to move on and serve God, too!' You don't need to be insightful to know that was not helpful, quite the reverse. It added substantially to the pain. In addition, it distanced the relationship. I felt misunderstood, I felt judged and as a result, I felt unsafe. In fairness to that individual, he later apologised; but the friendly fire had still hit home and done its damage. That conversation did me harm, not good. It had the effect of trivialising, even challenging, the authenticity of my mourning and my pain. And made an incorrect judgement about my appetite to serve God.

A friend of mine, a church leader himself, lost his dad in traumatic circumstances. Two weeks later – two weeks – one of the church members actually said to his wife, 'Are you over it yet?'

In another experience, there was a large church gathering where the leaders had asked a church member to give a testimony about a family member who was healed from bowel cancer. The very thing that only weeks before Joel had died from. It was all well-meant, but the pain inadvertently inflicted, and the shock for us sitting in the congregation, was still real. Another shell fired from a friendly gun found its target. In Appendix Two we have put together a short checklist for church leaders and pastoral workers to help avoid this kind of well-meaning but misguided friendly fire. All it needed was for church leaders to check if there was anyone for whom this testimony might be a challenge and then give that person the 'heads up'.

The leaders in this church were quick to apologise and a few Sundays later alerted us to an upcoming talk that they sensed might be painful for us.

Let's fix grief

There was one church where the elders talked to us after the *All About Heaven* event. They wanted to talk to us about one of their church members and in the conversation remarked, 'We have a lady who, every Christmas, near the time of the anniversary of her husband passing away, goes through a tough time and we don't know how to "fix it".' Gill's response was to say, 'How about instead of trying to "fix it", acknowledging this is a trigger point? Then, as elders, send her a beautiful card every year with some comforting words, reflecting back to her how much you care about her, how much her husband meant to you all? And assure her that you are praying for her during this period of time?' That's a very practical example of very well-meaning godly folk who inadvertently were adding to a widow's grief, now instead, seeing a way to be part of the promised Holy Spirit's comfort.

I remember too the big auditorium in France. Gill and I had presented *All About Heaven* and the Spirit of God was so very real in his comforting, healing presence. All around the auditorium there were scores of grieving people being prayed for. One church pastor came up to Gill and me and said, 'This lady will not stop crying. Do I let her cry and for how long?' You know by now what the answer was: 'For as long as it takes!' I was so grateful for this French pastor, who had the humility and the wisdom to know that he needed to check and didn't just go with his instinct to 'fix it'. What a beautiful thing that in the family of God this dear sister then felt comfortable enough to cry as long as she needed.

No tears here please

Christians often feel, or others incline them to feel, guilty or at least awkward over long-continuing tears of bereavement. Sometimes other well-meaning church members try to share scriptures to help us find peace or move on. Apparently, the comfort of the Spirit should be sufficient to dry tears. However, the fact is that the drying of tears does not fully happen until heaven, *QED*.

Perhaps the more like Jesus we are, the more we will be like Jesus at the tomb of Lazarus. We are allowed to weep, it is expected, and it's worth repeating he even gathers our tears into his bottle.[3]

We can actually add to the pain, distress or discomfort by being uncomfortable or impatient with grief. Nowhere in Scripture does it suggest that comfort ends or removes grief. It's important we get this, so that we can give others space to grieve, knowing they are safe with us. And more importantly, maybe, just maybe, we can learn what it is to be a conduit of comfort, discovering in the process how the blessing of those who mourn might involve you and me!

In one of the more extreme examples of this, at a funeral a well-meaning pastor went around and based on the scripture 'he gives the oil of joy for mourning',[4] offered prayer for people to find joy.

An older, mature leader took the pastor aside later and made it clear that albeit with the best of intentions this pastor had not allowed people to grieve. He made the point,

'You have taken one scripture and misapplied it and ignored the more appropriate scripture which would have been "a time to weep [and] a time to mourn".'[5]

Oblivious to the pain!

I was chatting to two friends whose family went through horrific child abuse, along with a number of other children in their church. Their grief was profound and deep. At one point, a respected national church leader said to them, 'Now you've got your life message!' Trying to 'enforce a spiritual outcome' on the most outrageous of all grieving experiences. The pain caused was enough to make these two friends to want to use bad words. How very, very wrong, how trivialising was that!

Thoughtful and wrong

We had many Christian folk trying to give us words of comfort, trying to give us scriptures, trying to pray for us. For example, a long-standing close friend and pastor came round in the early days, desperately wanting to help, and I think was shocked that I would not even see him. Why was that? Well, for Gill at that point in her journey with grief, talking to others was a genuine comfort, it allowed her to pour her heart out. For me, it was damaging; it was not a comfort, it was very different. It stirred up unimaginable pain that I couldn't process. 'Each heart knows its own grief.'

Sensing my friend's discomfort, I said to him, 'Look, I understand you mean well, but I can't deal with this. I'm very happy, after you have spoken with Gill to join you, for you to pray for us, but I can't engage in conversation.' Now, that wasn't remotely a bad experience, but it's an example of how 'each heart knows its own grief' and how each person will respond differently.

Thoughtlessness and carelessness

I remember it as if it were yesterday. Gill and I had plucked up the courage to attend a conference. It was a few months after Joel had died. We were ultra nervous about it because of the almost inevitable emotional turbulence it would stir up. We were sat in a lounge area with a cup of tea, and some folks came to join us, trying to reach out and talk.

From the outset it didn't feel a 'safe' conversation for me; the barriers began to go up. I think instinctively I have come to know when a person is not really engaged. It's rather like they are trying to do the right thing but somehow not properly given to it. It's as if it's a Christian duty 'tick box'. A moment when I can tell my conscience that it is a caring moment, but the reality is it is not a vulnerable, fully engaged, heartfelt engagement.

Suddenly, with almost zero warning, one lady jumped up and said, 'I can't wait to see my son. I haven't seen him for months!' and ran off to greet him. Innocent but oblivious to the broad-headed arrow that pierced our hearts!

Different readers have articulated their experiences to Gill and me, and a number have described that one of the hardest things was having their grief minimised. Others have related to us that friends have compared their marital break-up, suggesting it was worse than widowhood because of the uncertainty – the not knowing why, or whether there was still hope, and implying that the widow was at least aware of the finality of their situation and could 'move on'!

The time it takes

Often, it's not so much the words themselves, but the way in which they are said, and more significantly, the moment in which they are said.

You cannot rush those who grieve and, by definition, you cannot rush caring conversations.

I shared my heart and risked my tears with one church leader. I even volunteered some deeply painful memories of a birthday sunrise faced alone. For me it was trusting, risky, and at a very deep level. The church leader came across rushed, quickly asking me if he could pray and he missed it by a mile. The pastoral visit left me feeling foolish and my vulnerable sharing undervalued and rushed.

In another situation I was daily at Joel's hospital bedside watching him going through the most brutal of treatments. With shock after shock of unimaginable proportions experiences that no parent should ever have to face. In the middle of this, one friend texted me 'If you want a beer or a glass of wine do shout'. It was simply a rushed communication for him but coinciding with a moment of deep trauma and pain for me. For whatever reason it left me reeling at the apparent trivialising of my pain. I know his intent was good, but it was rushed and the disconnect was hard to bear.

Avoidance

Several members of our family have been in their local town centre and seen church members quite literally cross to the other side, head down, trying to avoid the need to engage in conversation. On one level I get it, people are busy-minded when shopping, and don't want to stop and probably instinctively know that to stop and chat is going to take a change of gear, a shift of pace and space. However, the end result was another burst of friendly fire scoring a hit.

A good friend of ours wrote the following:

> We had only been married a few years and had some very good friends who were having their first baby. We were delighted for them and were

ready to celebrate the birth with them. However, the baby died a few hours after birth. The mum was still in hospital as people didn't get discharged so quickly in those days. They were obviously devastated. Likewise, we were also shocked.

It was the first time we had been close to a situation like this, and we just didn't know how to handle it. Consequently, we stayed away from them because we didn't know what to say or what to do. It was some time before we were able to confess to them how we had mishandled the whole situation – they forgave us, and the friendship has survived other subsequent traumas in life.

A short time later, some other friends went through a stillborn birth. This time, we were much better prepared, and were able to be there with them, listen to them talk, and grieve with them, and not try and fix it. A lesson learned the hard way (like so many others in life!) but worth its weight in gold.[6]

The language of grief

One of the challenges for those trying to love and help those who grieve is that we don't have a language. It's like being in a country where no one speaks English, and we have no idea what to say and how to ask questions. We also run the risk of saying something without any idea of the anger, embarrassment or misunderstanding it can cause. Worse still, there's no Google translate equivalent to help us out.

In the next chapter I am going to give some suggestions around language that heals, language that helps and language that understands. In this chapter my hope is to share examples of where language can potentially damage. In other words, to paint a picture of the key dangers to avoid and more than that, to try and point to a way of thinking and being which will lead to better, more helpful outcomes.

Moving on?

One of the most common and damaging phrases used by caring people is the notion of 'moving on'. If you want one phrase that is an absolute 'no no', then this phrase probably tops the list.

Author and speaker Nora McInerny writes:

> I haven't moved on and I hate the phrase so much and I understand why other people do because what it says is that my husband's life and death and love are just moments that I can leave behind me.
>
> For those left behind, moving on implies that their loved one is not important, their loved ones can be forgotten. It is trivialising all that they have lost and trivialising the one they have lost.

> Some people assume that grief is a bad bout of flu to be got over in a matter of weeks, months or even days. My work colleagues were thinking OK, you've done that, now move on.[7]

The next chapter will provide some alternatives, but if there are to be one or two meaningful and lasting takeaways from this chapter, then my hope is that 'moving on' will be on that list as one to avoid.

A language primer – what to avoid[8]

- Please don't tell people who are grieving to read Job!
- Please don't say: 'You should be over it by now.'
- Please don't give pat answers to difficult questions such as: 'I don't know where my mum is now.'

A language primer – real life examples of sentences that should never have been said

- It wasn't cancer that killed Joel, it was the morphine, that's how they knew how long he had.
- Have you seen him yet?
- The Olivers need to know Joel's in heaven.

- Your son was into killing for sport, Scripture takes that seriously and there are serious consequences in Scripture.
- I understand what you are going through.
- I cannot understand what you are going through.
- My brother has just been sectioned.
- I lost my dog.
- What door did you open?
- Was she involved in sin?
- God must know that you're strong enough to handle this.
- He is in a better place.
- Time will heal!!!!
- You've got permission to marry again.
- You're young, you'll get married again.

Language primer – readers comments

- It didn't help me when leaders said to me that I must go to church and get into worship. It just brought condemnation because I genuinely couldn't.

- Just after the funeral a Christian lady came up to me and asked, 'Was your husband saved?' How insensitive and inappropriate. I felt so angry.

And just so that everyone reading knows that I get it wrong as often as anyone else! One of my worst blunders was to write the book *All About Heaven* without getting input from Joel's family; and in addition, putting into that book the statement, 'Joel wouldn't come back even if he could.' That was deeply damaging. It caused great pain.

Chapter Seven

Help That Heals

It may be that the previous chapter has left you feeling uncertain of how to help in a way that heals. On one level it's fairly simple and in this chapter, we explore some practical ways and some important keys in helping well.

The starting point

Thinking back over the thirty-plus *All About Heaven* events and recalling the shock we faced after the first event, when about 10 per cent of the room came forward to talk about their stories of grief, at each subsequent event we were better prepared and no longer surprised. What continued to surprise us, however, was the nature of those conversations. Inspiring and anointed as I think most of those evening events were on the topic of heaven, most people came forward because for many of them, it was the first time they had been able to talk about their loss with anybody in a church setting. It was almost as if they were saying, 'Thank you for your talk on heaven; it's amazing and wonderful for our loved one, but please can we talk to you about our loss?'

The range of conversations has continued to surprise us. We had multiple conversations where family members had died from suicide. I will never forget the first conversation of its kind. We were at a large family camp being hosted by the main leader. He and his wife have been close friends for decades and we know them as extraordinarily gifted and faithful, caring pastors. We did the talks on heaven, and one of the first conversations afterwards was from a long-standing church member, who had experienced a suicide in his immediate family. Our pastor friend was shocked; he had no idea!

In one church in the mid-West, we had a steady stream of deeply moving stories. One grandma had the shock of her eight-year-old grandson playing in a grain silo when the grain mound collapsed, and he was buried underneath. Another couple had lost two sons. One had died after being knocked off his bike. The other, a teenager, was cutting the grass on a sit-on mower. The mower had rolled down a hill where he was trapped and died. This was understandably deeply, deeply distressing. They confided that they had never been able to share their loss in a church setting. The dad had shared it with one or two other men. This was and is a good church, a caring church, and yet the leaders had no idea! In fact, the leaders shared with us that they had an awareness that something wasn't right and had been praying, looking for a conversational door to open into this family.

Another conversation was with a man whose brother had killed his wife and children and then killed himself. In another church, one of the church elders had experienced assisted suicide in his family. These are deeply distressing and painful loads these individuals were carrying. In every case the churches were and are caring churches, and yet for most of the hundreds of people we prayed with, they felt unable to share in their church setting. For many, sharing with us was the first time they had been able to unload their grief.

Thinking and reflecting on this, I have asked the question, 'Why?' And the answer on one level is fairly simple. During the evening event, Gill and I share our own loss, and in the process, there is an inevitable vulnerability. Little surprise, then, that these folk felt safe to tell their story to us. They knew we would give them time and space. They knew we would understand, and boy, did they want to tell us their story. In every case, they wanted to give their loved one a voice, they wanted their loved one's name to be heard, to be cried over. They wanted to be embraced and for others to validate the deepness of their individual loss.

Validation

I recall an unexpectedly tender moment. I was visiting an office to pay a bill and the manager asked how I was. I hesitated and yet something in this man gave me the courage to open up a fraction. And I felt the gently growing sense of validation when this manager cried openly in the office as I told him about Joel's death. The work around him paused, and even though it was an open-plan office, he stopped and engaged with me. He gave me time, asking me caring questions; and with every answer to his questions, more tears seeped from the corner of his eyes. He knew me a little, we weren't close friends, I was a customer. But something in his approach felt safe, felt loving, felt validating. I would have shared any detail with him that day because I could sense the validation of my grief, I could sense unrushed time, and it did me good.

Not long after Joel's death, two Jewish business colleagues, Bob and David, called me. In both instances I was driving, and I wasn't taking any calls at that point. But for some reason, albeit reluctantly, I took their calls. I was surprised by their seemingly effortless and natural ability to empathise. They were comfortable engaging with my grief. It wasn't awkward for them. I chatted to them years later to try to understand how they could do what very few others had managed to do. What became clear was that they understood the notion of standing with others in great pain. Bob said, 'I know there are no words that can truly help.

You are my friend, my desire was simply to be there and try to help and to try and heal.' They both talked openly about Joel, they named him without awkwardness, his business successes, his family. They used phrases like, 'I know there are no words to describe what you are experiencing but I am here'; 'I know your pain is unbearable'. As Bob said, we don't have the language to describe the unbearable. Somehow, they both knew how to validate my pain and my emotion, and they understood the importance of that validation. And, no surprise, they did me good.

I see your pain

Gill learned from our *All About Heaven* evenings talking to grieving folk at the end, one phrase that seemed to consistently help is the phrase, 'I see your pain.' It's not a silver bullet but it is a safe phrase to use, providing it's true when spoken. The reason it is helpful is because it validates the person's grief, mourning and pain, without trying to fix it.

The Jewish protocols and traditions for mourning are also really helpful. One tradition is the tradition of Shiva where for six days, every day, friends, neighbours and synagogue members would visit to bring food and to offer condolences. On the Sabbath, close family alone would attend. Those grieving sit on lower chairs and tear some part of their clothing. I reflected that this is their lifestyle, so hardly surprising then that Bob and David were at ease with me.

Daily prayer services, including the recitation of the *Kaddish* (a prayer that sanctifies God's name), are held in the home. The community plays an active role, offering support, bringing food and caring for the mourners' needs, reinforcing the Jewish value of *hesed* (kindness).

Support is the 'done thing'; it's what you are expected to do. As David put it, 'Not to go would be frowned upon. If you speak to people in life, you should be there supporting in death.'

Reflecting on my questions about the process, David put it this way: 'There will always be someone who says the wrong thing. Some say the right thing, some say the wrong thing, and on one level, it doesn't matter. What matters is that everyone is able to chat openly about the departed loved one. How old were they? What did they do for a living? All this allows them to talk openly about the fact that someone has had a life and is no longer here.' There is something very reassuring and comforting about this structured and accessible expectation. And something very healing in all that taking place in a safe way in the home.

Aled Griffith is a church leader and friend. His wife, Helen, died from cancer and in the days that followed he wrote the following: 'The intervening time is a blur of lovingkindness and bucketloads of biscuits and deliveries of flowers that Kew Gardens would be proud.' He remarks:

'The first week we had three open houses in the afternoon so whoever wanted could drop in and have a cup of tea and give their best to us. It was not good to be alone. None of it was possible without the support of good friends who organised it all.'[1]

I loved the natural way that in the home, as Aled put it, people were encouraged to 'give their best to us'.

Super Validating Prayer

Dr Rob Parsons is a prolific author, speaker and founder of Care for the Family, a national charity in the UK. Over the years I have had the privilege of being invited to speak at some of the Care for the Family events and in the process, got to know Rob. When Joel died, Rob reached out to us and came to visit. He sat and listened for an hour and three quarters. He cried with us; he barely spoke and when he did, he shared a couple of metaphors, one of which Gill found particularly helpful. However, when Rob left (and even as I type this up six years later, I'm crying) he said, 'I did not know how to approach today; the only thing I could do was pray: "Lord, let me do them no harm."'

Those words had a comforting, compassionate power. The reason they carried an empathy, and a deeply meaningful impact, was because they came from someone whose heart was humble, someone who knew they didn't have the right words and someone whose prayer was all they could offer. They also came from an incredibly busy man with lots of demands on his time, who somehow gave us unhurried time, leaving us with the impression that for that one-and-three-quarter hours, we were the only thing that mattered to him.

That prayer brought the Holy Spirit's comfort. And his understanding in that prayer brought comforting validation in the pain. I remember thinking at the time, 'He gets it.' It did us good.

Time!

These examples of validation and others throughout the book all require time. None of these individuals 'had' time but they 'made' time. Give me time and I may feel safe with you, there is at least a good chance. And if we are going to 'weep with those who weep',[2] we need to understand that you can't rush tears. There is 'a time to weep', says the philosopher in Ecclesiastes 3:4 – notice that word? Time!

You will possibly recall that I am a sailor. A few months after Joel died, I was making myself face the prospect of my first sail without him. I love sailing but I was dreading this first outing. I knew I could not do this on my own, the thought alone was producing piercing pain; and yet finding the right person was challenging to contemplate. I thought of scores of possibilities and in the end, there was only one person. His name is Tom.

Tom had been a great church leader but for some reason found himself discouraged with church leadership and felt a leaning to move out of 'professional ministry' into the everyday world of work.

Left feeling raw and vulnerable and needing a job to support his family, Tom took some practical work with a local company.

He was wrestling with his own faith journey and partly because of that I knew instinctively he was the one person I could be safe with. He didn't have it all together. I knew he could handle me in any state; sobbing, angry, shouting or wailing. He would never slap a Bible verse on me, and he would give the one thing guaranteed to help me that day. Time. He was brilliant in every way and without any words he left me feeling better; he understood the magnitude of what I faced that day, didn't trivialise it or offer toxic positivity – he did me good.

Ecclesiastes 7:2 suggests, 'It is better to go to a house of mourning than to go to a house of feasting, for death is the destiny of everyone; the living should take this to heart.'

One of the most hurtful things I've found is when people's response to me is rushed. It's almost as if they nod towards my pain, but it's a superficial nod. It's not the holding of the hand or the arm round the shoulder. It's a glance of acknowledgement, but no more than a glance. I find that deeply painful, deeply difficult to handle. My pain is deep; shockingly deep. My loss is profound; it has left me to some degree feeling abandoned; reeling from the destabilising motion of it all. And caring validation is one of the most precious, priceless, positive things that you can give me.

With this thought in mind, someone wrote to Gill and me about a neighbour who had lost two members of the family:

> I spent a lot of time with her, just being. If she wanted to talk, she did and if she wanted to cry, she did. It has remained in my mind ever since how one day she said to me that she had lost her friends in that they didn't know what to say or do. She said if she met folk when out, they would avoid her. She said I was the only person who would come near her if she cried. If she opened the door to a visitor and she looked as if she had been crying or was upset, they made excuses, they left. I have never understood that. I just sat with her or held her and let her be herself and let it out.[3]

I am so aware that none of us consciously wants to cause pain. However, we find ourselves avoiding the bereaved and it's often because we don't know how to heal the one grieving, nor do we know how to dry their tears and help them move on. But that's precisely the point. Right then I don't need healing, I don't need you to wipe my tears away, and I am certainly not ready to move on. More often than not, I don't need to hear any of your words. So let me encourage myself and I hope, encourage you, to seek out ways to be present.

Help without words

Someone who I barely knew, but who knew of my situation, gave me a hug but left it at that, minimal words. That was what I needed.

> The friend who can be silent with us in a moment of despair or confusion, who can stay with us in an hour of grief and bereavement, who can tolerate not knowing, not curing, not healing and face with us the reality of our powerlessness, that is a friend who cares.[4]

Job's comforters were of some use when they kept quiet and sat it out with him. When they spoke, it produced torment, anger and deeper grief.

Kessler offers a simple but profound insight: 'The need is for someone to be fully present to the magnitude of their loss without trying to point out the silver lining.'[5] Our presence needs to be just that and often only that. Our full presence, no distractions, fully present, not glancing at our phones, not looking around the room. Fully present, direct eye contact, and where appropriate, a physical touch; a hug.

One of my pastoral friends reminded me of the story of Ezekiel. In chapter 3, Ezekiel is told to eat the scroll and then to sit for seven days without saying anything. My friend describes it like this: 'To sit where they sit and feel what they feel for seven days. You don't impose your views, asking questions as to how they're feeling and then telling them everyone is going through this. At that moment sharing similar stories misses it by a mile. Better to identify with where they are and avoid the temptation for superficial positivity or trying to fix it!'

However you process that thought, the one thing that is obvious is that it took time!

People often describe the process of grief as if their world has stopped while everyone else's world is carrying on as if nothing has happened. That is why being present, having time, being engaged without a deadline or without something else to do or somewhere else to go is essential. For the grieving person, time stands still, and if you or I want to help, we had better understand that, and in that understanding, stop our own world with all its pace, all its demands and priorities, and give our fullest presence.

Say their name

One of the things I have noticed with nearly all the interactions that were helpful for Gill and me is that along with validating our pain and grief, Joel's name would be spoken. *What would Joel have done here? What made him laugh? Joel would approve of this, wouldn't he?* Hearing others talk or ask about our loved ones and hearing their names spoken, and then having the chance to share a little about them and their lives is rare, and is so valuable when it happens.

Another reader wrote to Gill and me:

> A lady I met asked me my daughter's name when she heard about our loss. She then wanted to know about her. It made me so happy to know that someone was interested in her and her life. It always seems strange to me that when you lose both parents, you are an orphan, when you lose a spouse, you are a widow or widower, but when you lose a child, there is no word for it. The way to handle grief is different for everyone, I realise. But I certainly find it a great comfort when people are interested in the life of the loved one. I don't want her to be forgotten just because she's not here with us now.[6]

How to help

I have already mentioned that I don't find it easy reaching out to a bereaved person. I often simply don't know what to do for the best. Rob Parsons' prayer has become a habit-forming prayer for me now: 'Lord, let me do them no harm.' And on a practical level, I would love to take some pressure off. Like me, you will almost certainly get it wrong sometimes, and yet if we can at least learn enough to make us more confident in helping others, that would be a great asset.

Asking the person with loss how they would like you to engage can sometimes help. I recall early in our marriage and with one child of our own, Gill and I moved into a house with a recently widowed mother, with two children and a baby. The local church small group had been faithfully supporting this lady and her late husband through his illness. They were exhausted, and they needed a break from the long-term intensity of care. For her it was unimaginable loss, unimaginable pain and here we are moving in 24/7.

Gill recalls, in the uncertainty of how we should operate, sitting down and saying, 'I have never been this way before, you will have to help me help you.' Another friend asks, 'Would you like me to talk or not talk, walk or sit?' You'll remember I mentioned the cat flap. For some members of the family it has been helpful to ask one another, 'Are you up for a cat flap moment?'

Little children show the way

We try our best to protect little ones from the worst of moments, from the deepest of expressions of grief, and rightly so. But don't be surprised if little ones show us what healing help does look like.

My friend Roger Greene tells the story of the death of his wife, Vicky, in the book *Dancing When the Lights Go Out*:

> My granddaughter Annie watched in sorrow. She hadn't experienced a family death before; the whole process was very emotional. Annie was observing silently, but when she saw me overwhelmed and my tears flowing, she came and sat with me, holding my arm, not speaking but looking me in the eye, her eyes full of tears for my pain. She didn't have the words, but she had the emotional awareness to touch and comfort me giving me her full attention.[7]

Around one year after Joel's death, I was out sailing with a work colleague and his family. Lovely, kind people, not churchgoers. I found myself getting tearful as memories unbidden began to surface and to avoid embarrassing anyone, I took myself off alone, to one side of the boat to reflect and to try to compose myself. I felt the gentlest touch on my shoulder and a little six-year-old girl's voice said, 'I do love you, you know.' No judgement, no clever words, not trying to fix me, just a wonderfully tender moment of kindness that healed something that day.

Sometimes the boil needs lancing

One of my friends lost his wife in the most harrowing of circumstances. He discovered the body and had to deal with police. The shock and trauma were severe. He had young children to take care of and needed to keep it together.

The question for carers then is: How do we handle something like this? One of his pastoral friends turned up and asked him, 'Have you been able to tell anybody the full story?' He then asked my friend to tell him every detail. Talking it out with someone, getting it out of our heads and sharing it with someone trustworthy so that at least one trusted person has the whole story, and all the detail has been vocalised, can be very healing.

My friend has subsequently counselled hundreds of people in his decades as a senior pastor. People who have died in hospice, people who have died from heart attacks and accidents, and his counsel is to get the bereaved at some point on the journey to vocalise the whole story. He remarks that in his experience, most bereaved folk have told their story in part and in fragment, but an element of healing is facilitated when they are able to tell it all.

Practical help that heals

One of the extra unwanted and unavoidable weights that lands on the shoulders of those who grieve is that practical life has to go on. In the very early days, when funerals, cremations or burials, finances, notifications, communications are almost ceaseless in their demands, there is an immediate need for most people to have practical help. Making sure meals are offered and delivered. Checking things like transport and accommodation for visitors. Maybe even helping a distressed newly widowed mum with the children. That might be buying clothes, school needs . . . the list is endless. Having someone else think this through and offer the help that is needed is a weight-lifting comfort.

In the context of grief, Paul talks about the depressed and sinking being cheered by the arrival of others.[8] That arrival is about practical help.

One of the things that many readers shared with us was that people would 'offer' to do a meal, cut the grass, go for a coffee and then just not do it. It's as if they either forgot or maybe just felt awkward in their own ability to handle the grief conversation potentially involved, and so retreated. Many readers talked to us – with some pain – of offers made at the funeral to help, but offers that simply evaporated. Life gets busy and people just forget.

Gill makes the point of asking, 'When can I bring a meal? When can we get a coffee? What would be the best time to XYZ?' 'Being specific,' she says, 'makes it a committed action and importantly, takes the weight of responsibility off the one grieving.' Don't be afraid to ask what specific help would mean the most, and if you do offer, please fulfil whatever it is you offered to do.

Here's a list of some practical, helpful suggestions that have demonstrably helped those who grieve:

- pick up prescriptions
- cut the grass
- pick up groceries
- provide a meal
- helping to reschedule appointments, e.g. hairdresser
- take a cake
- sort out flowers that have been given (change the water; maybe bring some disposable vases)
- refuel the car and check the tyres
- walk the dog
- wash the car
- fix things in the home
- find out what the children want or need, and make sure there's practical help there
- include children with other children

- taking widows or widowers out for coffee or afternoon tea, especially on bank holidays and anniversaries

NB: A checklist for church leaders and pastoral workers can be found in Appendix Two.

Chapter Eight

Unanswered Prayer, Unanswered Questions and No Regrets

For those struggling to make sense of life with no faith and no God, death, grief and the subsequent loss can be seemingly unbearably overwhelming. But for those with a faith, other challenges present themselves in particular in the shape of unanswered prayer and unanswered questions.

In the book, *Faith Questions in Bereavement*, Yvonne Tulloch says:

> Unresolved questions are okay. The questions we can have in the wake of bereavement may be resolved quickly or they may linger for years. Some of us may take a long time to really value our faith in the light of experiences. It's likely though that our faith will show the marks of bereavement and be forever changed.[1]

Ultimately, we may have to accept there is no answer to some of our questions. 'Man is born to trouble as surely as sparks fly upwards.'[2] Most families at some point will experience trouble in many forms, including trauma, grief and deep pain, where foundations get shaken, and people will ask many questions like, 'Why do I feel this way?' or 'Why do I feel God has let me down?'

After a brutal, untimely or traumatic death of any kind, it's almost inevitable that most will find their confidence in a loving protecting God at the very least tested or shaking.

The Secret Deal?

How do I keep trusting God and believing what Scripture says when trusting in God at that moment seems the opposite of reality? Questions surface without being asked, and they will force their impolite and unrestrained way to the surface. *If God is real, why would he do this to me? How could He let my son suffer such brutal pain and such torturous interventions?* I trusted God to answer my prayers, and I felt abandoned.

In reality this is, in part at least, a reflection of what many Christians believe is the Secret Deal. If I am a churchgoing Christian, I know I'm going to get hit with small things like flu or financial pressures, but the Secret Deal means I really am not expecting to lose a child, or have a loved one diagnosed with incurable cancer, or lose my home.

It's quite possible that in our hearts we may well have believed for or hoped for something that however we clothe it, is the Secret Deal. The truth in Scripture, as in life, is that there is no Secret Deal, even though our theology may not have grasped that fact.

However, there are times when the desolation of prayers not answered with a 'yes' carries great pain, great sorrow and distressing outcomes. After Joel died, and even during his treatments, this sense of distress and desolation was dark and crushing. At these moments the anguished cry of 'Why?' can burst from our souls and quite likely not find an answer this side of eternity. And I wanted to acknowledge there will be some for whom this is a painful reality right now. I also wanted to say, as someone who has journeyed this road, God knows, really knows and God cares, really cares.

It's common for those with a faith to feel a sense of abandonment, we feel so utterly alone. The God of love and goodness who could have changed the outcome is noticeably silent. It helps to know that even Jesus can identify with, understand and empathise with these deepest of feelings. In the garden of Gethsemane, he cries out, 'My Father! If it is possible, let this cup of suffering be taken away from me. Yet I want your will to be done, not mine.'[3] On the cross we hear his deep sense of abandonment: 'My God, my God, why have you forsaken me?'[4]

At the very least that should reassure us that Jesus himself understands the pain of unanswered suffering and unanswered prayer and, importantly, understands the pain of feeling abandoned by a God we have trusted.

A perspective on prayer for healing

The reality is that some prayers for healing get answered with a 'yes' and some do not!

I have one friend whose wife contracted cancer in her face. He prayed for her three times and then left it with God. She was healed. The same friend had a daughter who died of cancer and prayers for healing were not answered. How do you even begin to process that?

In a well-known scripture Paul says, 'Three times I pleaded with the Lord to take it away from me. But he said to me, "My grace is sufficient for you, for my power is made perfect in weakness."'[5] Paul prayed for healing, but God answered with grace instead of removal of suffering. God left Paul in weakness so that his power could be demonstrated.

There is not a single prayer prayed that goes unanswered. Sometimes it's 'yes', sometimes 'no', and sometimes something gets worked into us that changes us, and that is the answer. The problem is in the process of grief that notion can add to the perceived cruelty of the process.

For the record, I do believe in prayer for the sick and I do believe in prayer for healing but not without some caveats.

Some Christians suggest that if we have faith or more faith, our loved one will be healed. That is a doubly crushing notion for those whose loved one dies. Others suggest it's because of sin in our lives or our loved one's life that healing doesn't get released. Or maybe we should do something or not do something for the person to get well. As a result, some tender-hearted, godly people are left feeling guilty, responsible and condemned.

There are places like the book of James where it says, 'Is anyone among you ill? Let them call the elders of the church to pray over them and anoint them with oil in the name of the Lord. And the prayer offered in faith will make the sick person well'.[6] But any exploration of that passage will reveal that the text is not just describing an instantaneous physical healing, it's describing a process of wholeness. And also, if healing does happen, are we to expect it again and again? Sometimes we're so keen to pray for healing we don't prepare people for death or grief. Every person Jesus healed ultimately died. Each person he raised from the dead ultimately would die again! Every person responding to James 5 and receiving some form of healing has ultimately died. And nowhere in Scripture does it promise that every prayer for healing would be answered in the way we want.

I suspect that this emphasis in the charismatic and evangelical world on pushing for, striving for, healing every time and for everyone, is one of the reasons why unhelpfully we have so little said about dying, about grief and mourning, to prepare everyone for the one unshakeable promise in Scripture that 'people are destined to die'![7]

In my years as a church leader, I have seen a number of gifted, charismatic, godly leaders die young. I watched as the whole church was involved in daily prayer and in days of fasting over many months. I watched as well-meaning prophetic words were given stirring false hope for healing, and yet in the end, God took them home. The church was exhausted from the prayer and fasting, and the shockwaves of apparently unanswered prayer left scars and questions for many. I get it. We are exhorted to ask and keep on asking and yes, there is a place for persevering, healing prayer, but somewhere in it all, his 'lovingkindness is better than life'.[8]

Handling the present in the light of a bigger picture

Earlier we saw Jesus crying out for the cup of suffering to be removed, and yet he also added, 'not my will, but yours be done'![9] He understood that God's will, God's kingdom was bigger than the immediacy of suffering. We look at the orphaned children, the widowed wife, the broken-hearted parents, and at that moment, those are all we can really see and feel. At that moment, we cannot begin to comprehend why God would allow that grief, that brokenness, that pain.

And on one level, death should never be. Death was never the plan of the Creator. And of course, none of us relish the thought of dying. Seeing loved ones die in some trauma or from a short or long illness is shocking to us. Instinctively we recoil. 'How can this be?' is our instinctive response and in that moment at some deep level we know that death was never the plan or the intent at creation.

So of course, we recoil and often find ourselves gasping with shock and pain in the middle of it all. The reality that it is 'better by far' for our loved one can easily be overwhelmed by the weeks, months and years of suffering and loss, that we as the bereaved are left to live with.

From day one right up to his last breath, Joel was positive, courageous and selfless in his attitude. He prayed daily for a miracle of healing, 'If he heals me, I will dance on the streets of Darlington,' but equally was ready and willing to go if his Maker should call him. As mentioned in Chapter Two, he told us, the family, that we would have to make peace with cancer.

Once or twice, when he felt totally at the end of any physical, emotional or spiritual strength, Joel said that he felt a lion roar from within his deepest being. Not something he had looked for, prayed for, or experienced before. Of course, the lion became a metaphor for the presence of God in the darkest moments, the strength of God in the weakest moments, and the sovereignty of God in the most hopeless moments.

We faced several medical procedures, one of which was very difficult and extraordinarily painful and left Joel and us reeling. On one particular day, Joel had wondered if he should still go for the offered chemotherapy – understandable with the trauma of the previous days of brutal interventions and his weakened state – as we prayed it through together, he looked up and said, 'Dad, we've got to give it at least one shot . . . I'll ride on the back of the lion and if I fall off, so be it.' One of the family suggested he visualise hanging on tight to the lion's mane and that brought a smile.

And so we came to the very last day. All of us were present when Joel went to his new home, quicker than any of us or the medical staff imagined. At one point he pulled down his mask and said, 'I feel so peaceful.' That made us grateful. Towards the very end he pulled down his mask and said, 'I think I'm going.' We read a few scriptures over him, and the very last words he heard in this life were these scriptures: 'Joel David, you have run the race, fought the fight, there is now a crown of life ready and waiting for you. Go get it . . .'

I think knowing in his heart that this moment would come, Joel wrote a poem and sent it to us just days before he left this world.

They don't control things
HE does

They can cut, inject and test
Playing with HIS masterpiece

Appearing to change shape and form
But it's already HIS plans and purposes

They book scans, X-rays and clinics
And yet HE is in total control

They struggle in the now
And yet HE is past, present and future

He is in Total control
He has already ordained it

Nothing has changed
HE is in control[10]

Does Scripture have the answers?

I don't intend to trivialise the pain that these questions often carry embedded in their asking. And having walked the path myself, I can assure you I'm not looking to burden anyone with unwelcome positivity. But to suggest that there are no glimpses of an answer in Scripture would be less than real. And I do understand that not all scriptures help everyone all the time, but there are some glimpses in Scripture that at the right time may just encourage you and me.

At some point in our grieving journey, if we allow it, Scripture will begin to come to our aid. But, and it is an important but, there is a timing here that is different for every individual. These scriptures are not a 'happy pill' that you can simply swallow at any stage of the grieving process. But they will in time become a safe and welcoming, comforting arm of strength that we can lean into.

One of my pastoral friends encourages those who grieve, if they can, to make space for Scripture, even the smallest amount as and when they can. He suggests that it gives space for what God may want to say. He reflects:

> I remember only too well when I lost my wife, six weeks after she died, I was reading Psalm 62, verses 11 and 12. 'One thing God has spoken, two things I have heard: that you, O God, are strong, and that you, O God, are loving.' It was as though God simply said, 'I'm strong enough to see you through, and somewhere in this, you will find the loving purposes of God.' It changed my perspective from bewilderment to faith; it didn't heal the grief, but a word from the Lord brought faith and peace.

As we have remarked elsewhere, some folks in their grief simply cannot read, so again this is not a one size fits all. But for those who can, maybe allowing some verses from the Psalms to accompany our journey will help. And if reading yourself is impossible, using an audio version of

Scripture or having someone else read it to us, for some at least, may bring the peace my friend describes.

It helps some people to know that when God calls our loved one home, it's because he has work for them to do. One of our *All About Heaven* evening events was in Fort Wayne, Indiana. We were talking to a church leader in the audience, her mum had died recently. She was in hospital, had suffered a heart attack and then another, and the doctor was making it clear if it happened again there was no more that they could do, and she would not be resuscitated. Her response startled her daughter. She said to the doctor, 'Don't worry, there are things I have to do that I cannot accomplish down here.'

The timing is never a mistake

'I am the Living One; I was dead, and now look, I am alive for ever and ever! And I hold the keys of death and Hades.'[11] He decides when the time is right. He decides when the lock turns. Satan's shadowy hand may be involved, but the Master, the Lord over death, controls the time, the process and the destination for every individual. Every family and every person will handle the moment differently. Some are ready to go, are at peace about it and know the time is right. They are just ready to give up the ghost, to yield their spirits into the hands of God. Others, like Joel and us, his family, will fight to the very end, look for healing, believe for healing. And if they should die in the process, is that failure? Is that some kind of lack of faith? Is that because of sin? Is it some great disaster from which the Church should reel in shock? No!

The moment Joel slipped into the next world, Satan wanted to shout, 'I've done it, I've got him.' Jesus proclaims, 'He is mine, all mine, safely mine, mine for ever.' Our grief, deep and painful as it is and will be, is temporary. From the very first minute, it was tinged with the colour of victory. As a family, with God's help, we will finish our own race to be run, we will climb our own mountains. But in eternal terms, it is such a short time, and then we will be with him again. Then there will be a whole new eternity of destiny and function to get stuck into together.

The healing ministry does not hold the keys of death and hell. The Church does not hold the keys of death and hell. Who does? An almighty, omniscient God, who knows everything right down to the deep stirrings of the orphaned child, the loneliness of the grieving spouse, the grown-up children who feel bereaved that their father or mother has gone in some way early.

Who holds the keys? An omnipotent God. All-powerful. He does release healing, but not to everyone and not in every situation. Even when healing is released, no matter how miraculously, every healed person who has ever walked this earth has subsequently died. Every person raised from the dead – and there have been plenty – still has to face the frontier of death. In the Gospels, Jesus raised three people from the dead – they still had to die! He knows the time.

Who holds the keys? A loving King who can't wait to welcome us home. A loving God who says there is a future beyond death that is far more wonderful and fantastic than you and I can even imagine – painful as the separation might be.

Our future existence is not in the hands of treatments, surgeons, miracle cures or their lack. My life is not in the hands of the gunman or the drunk driver. My life has always been and will always be in the hands of the Almighty. He will have the last word, he holds the keys, and he can and does determine when I take my last breath here and my next breath somewhere else. Ecclesiastes tell us, 'No man has power to retain the spirit, or power over the day of death.'[12]

'Why' may be the wrong question

After Joel's death there were the inevitable questions including the obvious one: Why? 'Why?' is a totally legitimate question. It's the most likely and most heart-wrenching of the questions that surface after loss. It's a totally legitimate question and yet it's a question that I've observed over the years rarely gets answered.

And while it is a totally legitimate question, it's one that frames the journey of grief in terms of: What is this doing to me? Or: What's the reason for the pain that this is causing me? Again, understandable and legitimate. But I wonder if focusing on the 'Why?' causes us to miss even more important questions, questions that God is ready, maybe even keen, to answer.

Over time a different question became important to me. What can I do that I could not do before? What could I do that I wouldn't have considered before? The difference is subtle but important. This is not about finding out the reason, but it is exploring what might be in God's heart for me. In my case, I committed as one small step in my response to research and write a book called *All About Heaven*, and subsequently this companion book. I appreciate that may seem a different kind of response and to be clear, I am not remotely suggesting that these books are the reason why Joel died. Never, not in a million years! That thought would trivialise his death and cause great damage to me and others.

I think in some small way, changing the question from 'Why?' to: 'What can I do that I could not do before?' or: 'What should I do that I wouldn't have considered before?' is a way of seeking first the kingdom of God[13] while travelling on my journey of grief. It's allowing God to work his purposes through me to do good. Not the answer to the most inevitable of all questions, but an answer that helps me in understanding my role or purpose on my unchosen journey of grief.

Elisabeth Elliot, who experienced widowhood at a young age, likely had this in mind when she wrote, 'He makes us wait. He keeps us on purpose in the dark. He makes us walk when we want to run, sit still when we want to walk, for He has things to do in our souls that we are not interested in.'[14]

No regrets

In his last weeks, Joel had been busy buying gifts online for members of the family for Christmas and beyond, and he also spent time thinking through and shaping several moments of carefully chosen words. They became Joel's gift of words to the family. One of the most helpful phrases, a phrase that Gill and I have leaned into, was: 'You'll get some things right and you'll get some things wrong but no regrets.'

The intensity of emotion and grief and the deep love we have can easily open a door that lets in condemnation and regret. And in many ways, regret is a natural response, an inevitable response to any loss. Our love for the individual will have us thinking of things we missed, words we never said, things we should have done and things we shouldn't have done. Decisions we made before they were ill or even while they were ill. It's so easy to slip down the steep slope called regret.

Rob Parsons articulates this in his deeply moving book *A Knock at the Door* describing the moment when Ronnie

Lockwood, who had lived with the Parsons family for forty-five years, was approaching the end of life:

> I went to the window and looked out. A path skirted the building and people hurried along it. In the far distance I could see cars on the motorway. I turned and looked at Ronnie lying in the bed. I suddenly had a deep desire to do something. Lemn Sissay wrote, 'If the adults don't care to hug a child, why should he feel huggable?' I walked over to his bed, put my arms around him and held him close. I had not done that in all the years he was with us and I wished with all my heart I could turn back the clock. As I clutched his almost lifeless body, and with tears running down my face, I whispered, 'I love you, Ronnie.'
>
> We sat in the darkness for a while and then the door opened. It was Lloyd. He walked straight to the bed and kissed Ronnie on the cheek. He stood for a while looking down at him, then said, 'We had some fine snooker battles, my friend.'
>
> And then we all started crying again. I wonder if we were grieving not just for Ronnie's dying but for words we wish we had spoken, times we could have been kinder, frustrations that could have been brushed aside if only we had known that time was so short. And yet I think we also knew

> that was foolish. How could any of us live under that kind of pressure in the normality and stresses of family life? But of this we were sure: we had loved him. Perhaps if there had been no regrets, there would have been no love.[15]

Seventeen months after Joel's departure I found Gill in tears. She was anguishing over Joel's last night. Some of Joel's oldest and closest friends arrived as a group at the hospital. Joel somehow found enough strength to prophesy over each one and then said, 'Does anyone want to say anything?' The silence was heavy. No one spoke; I think the emotions were so painful none of us could find the words. Looking back, Gill wished desperately that she had said something. She was so very, very sad. She knew what it had taken for Joel to summon enough strength to deposit what he did. And she was doubly sad that after his sacrificial giving to each individual, not a single person, including herself, had been able to say anything positive to Joel or for Joel. Hurt for her son was a sword that pierced her soul.[16]

As I reflected, I said to Gill, 'Looking back now, we were all in grief, shock and trauma, surviving the moment. None of us were aware it was going to be his last night on this earth. And our pain was so acute, and our awareness that what he had said was important, we were hanging on every word desperately trying to make sure we didn't miss anything of significance'. Of course, she understood the logic but her pain in that moment was undiminished.

I was able to remind her that the following morning she had been able to share words with her firstborn son and was able to say, 'Joel, it's been a privilege to have you as our son.' That memory is deeply important and deeply meaningful.

There are always going to be 'if onlys'. With Joel's death there were many along the way, and even more at the very end. They are a natural response. But somewhere, at some point, whatever my pain and however intense my grief, my convictions will surface – Jesus really does hold the keys to death, and he is sovereign, and he really does have the last word.

Of course we will feel regrets, but as Rob put it so well, 'And yet I think we also knew that was foolish. How could any of us live under that kind of pressure in the normality and stresses of family life? But of this we were sure: we had loved him.'[17]

What did Joel mean when he said, 'You'll get some things right and you'll get some things wrong but no regrets'?

If Jesus holds the keys, and that means the timing too, then that timing can be trusted with the pain we carry of things not said, and of things not done. Yes, we will feel the pain of them, accept some things we did right and some things we did wrong, but we don't have to hold on to them and live with that pain. And if at any point those regrets are from some relational damage, let's forgive and live with no regrets.

Anthony Kelton was a close friend and pastor to Joel. His own daughter, Anna, died a few months before Joel's departure from an unexpected and distressing medical emergency. Still grieving Anthony now found himself facing the last moments on earth with a friend he loved. Turning to his creative gift he wrote these words:

The Burning Tree of Cancer

It was obvious.
His personal presence with all his history, was disintegrating!
Speeding toward too soon a Past!
Cancer was enlarging him.
Squeezing breathing out of him and fast closing down his earthly journeying.
Life was exchanging living existence for Farthest Distance,
into an insistent Other Realm.
Before Door opened entrance into death,
daily multiplied pills made him stronger,
whilst we, the tearful, the fearful living,
were able to converse a little longer;
delaying inevitability.
We the living, despise dying.
And so we would not and we could not, let dying go.

It was not obvious.
Revealed Truth is hardly believable.
Upon leaving chemotherapy ward
the slow dissolving beloved victim
hobbled after me.
Dying wanted to thank and encourage further
visitations.
To confront this unnecessary humility I turned
around to lovingly chastise,
and, another World confronted me!
A burning tree without burning.
Luminosity blazed complexion,
his dying face, glowing!
I was humbled backward into our past places,
into remembrances.
It ought to have been obvious.
Diminishing earth was losing him,
another world claiming him.
Something stronger than death,
transferring him!
Dying's transportation had arrived;
and he smiled!
It was his old smile and time for earth love
to separate.
Stunned, shocked, I blurted out:
'Are you leaving today?'

Obviously.
It has become obvious.
The whole startling experience was his very last, brave, disclosure to me.
To have observed this viewing, this mysterious sad delight
has become my daily mystery and daily memory,
observing darkness overcome by Light.

Anthony L. Kelton

Chapter Nine

God's Promises

The overarching backdrop to death, dying, grief and mourning is that the Bible speaks about it, faces it head-on, and validates the varying experiences of grief that different individuals have. And whatever our individual experiences, to help us all navigate the future, the Bible not only faces death, grief and mourning with reality, it also gives us promises to lean into, promises to stand on and promises that help us navigate our journey to still waters and green pastures.[1]

The promises of God

The Bible offers many promises of comfort, hope and peace to those who mourn the loss of loved ones. For some, it seems, the thought of church members dying doesn't sit well! That's especially the case when the church has prayed and maybe even fasted for healing; death appears as some form of defeat that church leaders especially would rather move on from! It's been said by many that the West has chosen to sanitise death; like a wet wipe wiping away unwanted dust from a house we want pristine.

Thank God Scripture is theologically and pragmatically different. Out of our journey, I want to share some well-known scriptures that can be a rock of promised comfort on which to stand during times of grief and the mourning process which accompanies it. I 'offer' these to you. I don't want to come close to imposing them on you. Yes, of course, every scripture is dependable and true, but not every scripture is helpful at every moment for everyone on their journey of grief.

Here are some of the key promises given to the bereaved:

Scripture One: He holds our hand

> I will take you by the hand and guard you.[2]

When you're in the dark or on the narrow path, you need someone to lead you by the hand, to hold your hand tight. You need someone to rely on.

God says we can rely on him:

> I've got you by the hand
> And I'll never let you go!
> No matter where you go,
> No matter what you do,

You always have
A hand to hold you.
I will lead you,
Guide you,
Keep you.
Even through death
I won't ever let you go![3]

Scripture Two: He is near in our crushed and broken state

The psalmist makes it clear: 'The Lord is close to the broken-hearted and saves those who are crushed in spirit.'[4] Incidentally, the individual is still broken-hearted and is still crushed in spirit, and this verse is not promising some immediate victorious healing, or liberation from those things. Those things, broken-heartedness and a crushed spirit, are a very real part of life. It's about letting the reality of the Lord's nearness do whatever he will do, and it will be uniquely different in timing, in shape and in practical experience for each one of us. And yet the same nearness also over time brings a binding up of those crushed wounds and a healing of the broken heart. Proximity! Even the word has a reassuring sound to it. It is so deeply meaningful to be reminded of his promise to be 'close', additionally reflected in the other scriptures we are considering.

Scripture Three: 'He heals the broken-hearted and binds up their wounds'[5]

Isaiah continues, 'The Spirit of the Sovereign LORD is on me, because the LORD has anointed me to proclaim good news to the poor. He has sent me to bind up the broken-hearted'.[6]

After loss, there will always be a missing piece in the jigsaw of our lives. At some point, the truth of Paul's declaration will make its mark: 'O death, where is your victory? O death, where is your sting?'[7] But please remember this scripture is not about healing grief, but rather giving us the ability to grieve with hope. So, yes, a victorious view of heaven removes the ultimate sting of death, but Psalms and Isaiah make it clear healing takes time. Our wounds are still wounds and those wounds need binding up.

Biblically, 'binding up' implies the start of healing, not its immediate completion. In ancient times, binding a wound was just the first step: to stop the bleeding, protect the injury and allow the body time to heal. So, in these verses, God's action is one of tender attention and ongoing care, not instant restoration.

Scripture Four: 'Blessed are those who mourn, for they will be comforted'[8]

As we explore here, Jesus did say 'blessed are those who mourn' and that is a rock-solid promise. However, those words are not a silver bullet, they are not a magic pill.

Here again we are careful. Not everyone who grieves can enter into the promise at every moment. It's possible for this verse to become an unhelpful pressure placed on us by others. But equally this promise is real, tangibly within reach and it can do us good.

The Holy Spirit is there in a unique way. He is there to be drawn upon. He is there to minister comfort. He is there to be sought out and readily found. He is there to speak to.

I can share a couple of examples that may help us get a glimpse of what 'comfort' looks like. The first is the day of the funeral or the Thanksgiving Service. There were many days of anticipatory dread for Joel's funeral. Carrying my son's coffin with Joshua, Joel's brother, and Jacob, Joel's son. Giving the eulogy, singing the songs, watching Joel's thirteen-year-old son stand by his dad's coffin and give a remarkable anointed eulogy of his own. But the presence of God that day was intense; it was evident for everyone, and was the only thing that carried our family through.

I could look back to the death of my mum, my dad, Gill's mum and dad, and the same dread at a very different level appears. I've done countless funerals as well on the other side; being the pastor, or the speaker, or the carer. And I can tell you, as probably you could tell me, the presence of the Holy Spirit bringing comfort for the family is almost irresistible, certainly irreplaceable, and the strength the Holy Spirit gives during that day, the capacity only the Spirit can give during that day with all the other colossal burdens, stresses and strains, is remarkable. In my experience thus far, it is an absolutely dependable, reliable outpouring of comfort. My mum at the funeral of my dad, like many before and after her, described it as 'like being wrapped in cotton wool'. I recall vividly at my dad's funeral, my broken-hearted mum singing the hymns with confidence, and with the beauty and clarity and pitch perfection of a song thrush at its morning best.

I've seen that look very different in funerals where there is no faith, where there is no Holy Spirit. Somehow, for those with faith, into all of that normal and natural emotion comes the anaesthetic of the comfort of God. In the process, somehow grieving takes on a positive dimension. It is a heaven-breathed process uniquely ours for this moment in which God's presence is somehow at its richest, its closest, its most real. On one level it should be no surprise, either. It is probably the one day in your life or mine when the most people from around the world are praying for us at the same moment in time. There is nothing more valuable on earth than the powerful, comforting presence of the Holy Spirit. If Jesus said it himself, most of us can find enough faith to believe it and ask for that comfort.[9]

So, the first level of comfort which is tangible, and everybody can get to see it, is a reliable, dependable presence of the Spirit's comfort and enabling for the funeral day. We can declare from experience that he is faithful, he will stand with us; we can expect to see an outcome.

However, after that day there's a journey, and everybody's journey is so different, another point on the journey where we lean into the biblical perspective that 'each heart knows its own grief'. In other words, grief is different for everyone, and so is the promised comfort.

There are moments in prayer and worship in which comfort simply comes. Through tears, through a silent invisible thread of strength, through the gift of tongues.[10] The comfort of the Holy Spirit will be direct and be immediate at times, and then ebb and flow over years, as it does; after all, the wind blows where it wants.

Sometimes the truth of Scripture will profoundly help. There have been many times on our journey that Scripture has been a rock on which to stand; a solid shoulder against which to lean. The fact that I have written, and you are reading, a chapter given over to promises in the Word of God is evidence of that.

However, having said that, the reality ebbs and flows.

Let me share three rather different moments of comfort, which may intrigue and/or surprise you. These are three things that have never happened before and have never occurred since.

The first vacation I was able to take with my second son, Joshua, after his brother had died, we were sailing along the south coast. As we came into the anchorage for the night, a single dolphin appeared. It played around our boat. Joshua got into our small dinghy and was able to be in the water for probably twenty minutes or more, almost in touching distance.

I can't tell you how or why, but the impact of that brought tears, brought memories and brought deep, deep comfort.

Our first wedding anniversary after Joel died, Gill and I were dreading the day, as I shared earlier. Somewhere around breakfast time, Gill and I were looking into the north-east corner of our garden and to our amazement, sat on a small shrub, there was a huge bird of prey. It stayed there from breakfast time till late afternoon.

I can't tell you how or why, but the impact of that brought tears, brought memories and brought deep, deep comfort.

In his own unique way, the Holy Spirit used the natural world. The fact that our heavenly Father cared enough to 'give us that very special moment' was comfort in itself.

Thirdly, I was away with Gill and again taking time out on our boat. Gill was fine, but I was in a very angry frame of mind. It was grief-related and I couldn't shake it. I got so agitated I had to get off the boat. I jumped into the dinghy and started rowing. I was still processing angry thoughts, anger at God, anger at others, when there was an unexpected moment of quiet, that seemed to come from nowhere; and I suddenly became aware of what my angry grief had shut my eyes to. In front of me, less that 10ft away, was a kingfisher on a branch. I sat absolutely still, and he let me watch him fish and eat twice before he flew away.

The anger dissipated like early morning mist in the heat of the sun.

And again, I can't tell you how or why, but the impact of that brought tears, brought memories and brought deep, deep comfort.

Again, the Holy Spirit used the natural world. And once more, the fact that our heavenly Father cared enough to 'give me that very special moment' was comfort in itself.

So yes, the Holy Spirit's comfort is found in many places, including Scripture. It ebbs and flows in all kinds of ways including the natural world He created and maintains; and sometimes it is brought to us in the guise of other human beings.

Scripture Four: God cheers us by the arrival of others

Paul describes it this way: 'But God, who comforts and encourages and refreshes and cheers the depressed and the sinking, comforted and encouraged and refreshed and cheered us by the arrival of Titus.'[11]

There have been a number of significant moments of comfort through the 'arrival' of others.

When Joel was in hospital and no diagnosis was forthcoming and the treatments were not being expedited, I reached out to a friend – former GP or family doctor now a church leader, Martin Dunkley. He was literally going through airport security when I called. He called straight back. And I'll never forget the weight-bearing load his words provided. He said, 'You are in my patch, and we will take care of you.' Martin helped us through the ups and downs of the hospital journey, helped us get some things moved forward. He and his wife, Lynda, made themselves available for prayer and through church members, provided accommodation and meals. In the bleakest of moments, Martin and the church provided comfort, encouragement and 'refreshment'. Honestly, I don't know how we would have 'hung on' in those bleakest moments without his 'arrival'. Following Joel's death, they supported us personally through the subsequent days, attended the funeral to support us and have remained close friends and prayer supporters in the seven years that have followed.

In the first week when we left Joel's family and returned home to Whitchurch, two friends dropped by with a meal. As I wrote this story, I found myself weeping. It was a small act and because of the circumstances, courageous. All I can say is that meal brought comfort. It wasn't the quality of the food (it was great), they had no words, it was the authentic act of kindness, Spirit-breathed kindness that brought comfort in itself.

Towards the end of our time with Joel, good friends of ours, Dave and Rachel, twice made the long journey of a 480-mile round trip. The first time they brought practical support, helping me meet advisors and helping our family. The sight of their car on the approach track to Joel's home was a deep comfort. It lifted our heads. Somehow their God-sent presence lifted the almost unbearable weight of responsibilities mixed with sadness. The second journey got all our children there by Joel's bedside with just minutes to spare so that they could be with their brother when he left this world for the next.

God who comforts and 'cheers the depressed and the sinking' sent Dave and Rachel, and several others.

Scripture Five: 'The LORD is my shepherd'[12]

The psalmist reminds us that 'Even though I walk through the valley of the shadow of death, I will fear no evil, for you are with me; your rod and your staff, they comfort me.'[13] The Hebrew rendering of that phrase is 'the valley of deepest darkness'.

Gill and I had the privilege of staying with two friends who housed us while Joel was in his last days, some of the deepest and darkest days to date, and helped us facilitate the twenty-four-hour family care that we gave to Joel. When Gill and I rang the doorbell at their home, we both crumbled, and for several hours our unstoppable tears provided the river along which we could push the boat of our questions, pain and uncertainties. Gill would say afterwards that it was as if we handed over all the broken pieces of the vase of our life and within those first few hours, they had glued them back together sufficiently to enable us to carry on.

It was these friends who explained to us (reflecting on this scripture) that grief is like a long black tunnel, pitch-black and with no apparent light visible at the end. Occasionally, it was suggested, just occasionally, you may see tiny pinpricks of light that last for a moment, a second or two. That's the biblical definition of grief, the valley of deepest darkness. And it's in that valley the Shepherd becomes so real.

The rod and staff are symbols that represent the proximity and compassion the Shepherd has for the sheep. The rod warded off predators; the staff was a guiding tool with a hook on one end to secure a sheep around its chest. Protection and guidance are promised, and an unmissable presence – the unmissable presence of God. Even when it seems so distant while still acknowledging the reality of your own broken-heartedness, this is something to hold on to, a rock to stand on. It's a pinprick of light in the darkness.

Scripture Six: 'Your lovingkindness is better than life'[14]

Earlier, I mentioned my father's death. I was twenty-one and had the privilege of nursing him with Mum. We had prayed and fasted and I had gone through stages of anger, sadness, fighting the seeming injustice, as I have previously shared here. The night he died, I was sleeping near him. When I woke up, I heard no breathing, looked across and saw death.

Shocked, I knelt at the foot of his bed, sensing the presence of God and his angels. And I found myself singing the words of our sixth scripture.

His lovingkindness is better than life. He said it; we can lean into its illuminating perspective. He said it; we can trust it.

Scripture Seven: 'The Lord gave, and the Lord has taken away; blessed be the name of the Lord.'[15]

This scripture is a tough one and not everyone finds this possible, especially in the early days. I was listening to an interview with worship artist Steven Curtis Chapman, talking about his album *The Glorious Unfolding*.[16] This album and much that he wrote and spoke about came from sharing the tragic loss of his child who was run over by a family member in the car right outside the home. He describes the pain as he woke up each day to the fresh awareness of loss. He found himself wondering if he would scream long enough and loud enough that his voice would go. He forced himself to say, 'Blessed be the name of the Lord.' And that's at the heart of this album.

We miss Joel. We miss his laughter, his generosity, his selfless care of us and others. We miss his love; we miss his irritating pranks. We miss his daily emails and his daily phone calls. More than I can ever tell you in words, like Tennyson, we long 'for the touch of a vanish'd hand, And the sound of a voice that is still.'[17]

But heaven has given our broken hearts a heart-warming hope: 'Then eyes with joy will sparkle, That brimmed with tears of late; orphans no longer fatherless, nor widows desolate.' There will be 'knitting severed friendships up where partings are no more!'[18]

On 20 December 2019 at 12.57, after my final words over Joel and as his last breath left him, these words were said: 'The Lord gives, the Lord takes away. Blessed be the name of the Lord.'

Goodnight, Joel, see you in the morning.

If that scripture may be a hard pill to swallow, a hard place to find, a hard truth to embrace, our last scripture will be like a healing salve, an irrepressible light in the darkest of places.

I have read this scripture many hundreds of times, but never really caught its depth until writing this book. Nearly seven years on from Joel's departure, I read with fresh eyes, fresh experience and fresh understanding our next scripture. Only in recent months has it sprung to my rescue.

Scripture Eight: 'The Father of compassion and the God of all comfort'

In familiar verses that carry a fresh and heartwarming illumination Paul writes 'Praise be to the God and Father of our Lord Jesus Christ, the Father of compassion and the God of all comfort'.[19] I have leaned into the reassuring shoulders of this scripture over and over.

It's a reminder of the reality that 'we cry "*Abba*, Father." The Spirit himself bears witness with our spirit that we are children of God'.[20] We can find moments when we simply lean into the wraparound love of the 'Father of compassion and the God of all comfort'.

And it's enough. Again and again, like a weaned child at his mother's breast, I have found this scripture a solid rock, a comforting shoulder, a reassuring presence. When David describes the weaned child in Psalm 131, it's the voice of someone who for that moment has ceased striving. The voice of someone who at that moment no longer feels the need to understand everything or to control outcomes. This scripture of the 'Father of compassion'[21] reminds me and somehow helps me enter the psalmists' experience and like a weaned child in those moments I know and experience that 'I am held'.

Scripture Nine: 'My desire is to depart and be with Christ, for that is far better'[22]

> What no eye has seen, nor ear heard, nor the heart of man imagined, what God has prepared for those who love him . . .[23]

As I have said before, when the Apostle Paul says it is 'far better', he is saying to you and me that the best of God lies beyond the grave.

C.S. Lewis articulated it like this:

> All their life in this world . . . had only been the cover and the title page: now at last they were beginning Chapter One of the Great Story which no one on earth has read: which goes on for ever: in which every chapter is better than the one before.[24]

God's eternity overcomes all sameness with infinite possibilities! Earth is not the best there is. It's wonderful, but it is less than, second string, not as good as all that is to come. Death is not the end of all that is precious, it's the doorway to the very best there is. Death is the doorway to the greatest adventure. Expect your God-given senses to reel and reel again as you travel to the next world and get to see perfect nature, perfect work, service or function, perfect art, design and construction and perfected relationships.

The best of God lies beyond the grave.

Chapter Ten

No Finish Line: Rebuilding with the Comfort of God

In preparing to write this book, I sought the input of friends and godly leaders who I have worked with over the decades. All of them to a man and woman were encouraging; keen that this book and its message be available for God's people. And interestingly, most of them (not all) were also keen that I ensured there would be chapter on 'Finding God in it all'. There was just the slightest hint that grief can hold people back from serving God or living a victorious life; or a hint that there should be a substantial healing from God for everyone who grieves.

I found myself reflecting on this sentiment. Is there a moment of healing, a new page, a new day, a new chapter, a new beginning? And what do we mean by those questions?

I couldn't find the right words to describe what this 'healing' looks like, and nor could I describe how you would know. Looking at things from another vantage point, it's helpful to be aware that there are barriers that potentially hold us back from fruitful, joyful life in God and living for God. But I think it would be wrong, deeply wrong, to suggest that for everyone who grieves there is a binary point when one moment you are not healed and the next moment you are. Leaning into the title of this chapter, I simply don't believe it's helpful to view the journey of grief as having a finish line that you cross and suddenly everything is back to normal or moved into a new normal.

I think the very fact it is not easy to put one definition, one word or even one sentence to clarify this stage of the journey is helpful in itself. What we are grappling with here is that my life is not defined by grief. Of course, my grief is valid, and of course, the love I have for my son is deep and the loss is still painful nearly seven years on. And as we have already stated, 'each heart knows its own grief' and as I have already said, losing both parents and parents-in-law is one thing; but losing my son, my best friend, my co-labourer in church and commerce is off the scale different. Equally, finding God and knowing a measure of healing is not a bull's eye on some target that we can all aim for, it too is different for everyone.

But the process of rebuilding is important, or as Elie Wiesel puts it, 'Let us remember Job who, having lost everything – his children, his friends, his possessions, and even his argument with God – still found the strength to begin again, to rebuild his life.'[1]

God wants to be present

Having said those things, I do believe – deeply – that God wants to be found in our grief. He wants to be present, involved, comforting, moving, working, dealing. In Chapter Nine we looked at the scriptures that promised comfort, that promised proximity to the broken-hearted, that promised healing, and that promise to bind up. But what does healing mean? If I have an amputated limb I can experience healing, but I still live, move, work and carry on with that loss. I will still walk with a limp. It's part of who I am, part of who God has moulded and shaped. Healing does not remove the reality of loss.

How do we find God in the midst of grief

The outcome of grief takes different forms: loss, isolation, depression, anger, doubt and questions. There's no way to avoid any of that. But that is no surprise to God and somehow, in the midst of grief and all its forms or manifestations, he wants us to find the healing that's only available in him. He wants to partner with us in the rebuilding.

One pastor friend of mine was telling me the story of a church member. This person had lost their partner in a tragic car accident and was left with four children to bring up. They said to my friend, 'I'm grateful for your pastoral care, and the care of the church, but when I shut the door, I have to get this from God.' They understood that however good the external support, ultimately they, and each one of us, has to find our answer, our healing and our peace with God.

And of course it should be obvious, God doesn't have a grief recovery template so that everyone can read the list, check off the boxes and find healing in some kind of linear fashion. The notion is silly but many live as if it were true.

Each heart knows its own grief journey too

We have already explored the notion based in Proverbs 14:2 that 'each heart knows its own grief'. It is equally the case that any measure of healing or restoration, rebuilding or recovery is also different for everyone. In this chapter I want to share stories that demonstrate how very different the journey and the outcome is for different people. Our first example is from Scripture and the story of Jacob. Here we learn that one individual can have two very different responses with two different types of loss in the same family.

One patriarch, two responses to grief

Jacob and his troubled family travel towards Ephrath from Bethel. As they were travelling, Rachel went into labour, but the day that was meant to be joy-filled – the second son of Jacob and Rachel being born – ended in devastation.[2]

Rachel, the beloved wife of Jacob, had at one time said to him, 'Give me children, or I'll die!'[3] After many years of barrenness she had her first son and named him Joseph, meaning 'may he add'. In a play on words, she then says, 'May the LORD add to me another son.'[4] God did just that, he gave her another son years later. However, the labour was hard, and Rachel struggled exceedingly. With her last breath, Rachel named her second son Ben-Oni,[5] meaning, 'son of my sorrow' or 'son of my pain'. Rachel received her wish of having two sons, but her life ended in childbirth.

Rachel was the love of Jacob's life, the girl he had worked fourteen years for, and it seemed 'like only a few days to him because of his love for her'.[6] Jacob determined that the loss of his loved one, and the deepest sorrow and pain would not have the last word in this situation. Jacob chose to rename his new son 'Benjamin', meaning 'son of my right hand'. The right hand was a privileged place, a place of honour; even today we say things like 'he's my right-hand man' to express particular care and love for someone. Benjamin was the son of Jacob's old age, and he loved him. Jacob refused to be defined by the sadness of the loss of his wife; instead, he redefined it by focusing not just on the loss, but also on the provision of God. And in this process, he renamed his son, and in that renaming there was a reframing enabling him to walk in the good of a healing process.

However, Jacob's response to the perceived death of his son Joseph was quite different:

> Then Jacob tore his clothes, put on sackcloth and mourned for his son many days. All his sons and daughters came to comfort him, but he refused to be comforted. 'No,' he said, 'I will continue to mourn until I join my son in the grave.' So, his father wept for him.[7]

This is the same man, with the same dependency on his God, who handled his two different moments of bereavement in two remarkably different ways. With one his beloved son there was no comfort enough, with the other, the love of his life, he chose to rename, reframe and rebuild.

Stories from others

In a church I have worked with for many years, one outstanding godly couple in leadership lost twins early in their marriage. Both girls died as babies in cot deaths about three months apart. When the second daughter died, the husband spoke to his wife and said, 'Shall we grieve like the rest of men, or shall we say like Job, "The LORD gave, and the LORD has taken away; blessed be the name of the LORD",[8] and walk on with him?'[9] And that is exactly what he did, trusting the Lord with his daughters, and giving God his grief. Not speaking of it again.

The journey for the wife was very different, compounded by being in a church in which no one spoke to her about what had happened for years. The unwritten expectation was that you just got on with life.

Several years later someone asked her if anyone had ever spoken to her or walked this huge double trauma through with her, she answered, 'No! In our church no one ever spoke about these things, you were just encouraged to get on with life.' She didn't choose this 'imposed' silence. She would have preferred to be able to share.

These are two very different, polar opposite ways of dealing with this trauma. One intentionally chosen and one essentially imposed. It didn't stop either of them from serving God together fully, they found strength in God, but the way they did that could not have been more different.

One reader wrote:

> My previously healthy man became extremely ill and after three hospitalisations in 2.5 months, he died. My mother died three months later and three other family members died in the next 1.5 years, ending with my daughter. Sadness became my companion, as the loss was overwhelming. I drew on my faith and realised I had to make a choice. Was I going to drown in sorrow, adversely affecting my job and relationships with family and friends, or was I going to immerse myself in my faith and seek my joy?

> Introspectively, I began to dwell on the blessings that were bestowed on me by those I had lost, focusing on all of the many great things/moments I shared with them, and I made a 'scrapbook' of these moments in my heart. I openly discuss the memories with my daughter and closest friends, and we often laugh about some of the crazy times. Did I cry? Of course ... I still do sometimes when something triggers a precious memory. But now my tears are tears of joy, of remembrance, and the gift of both. I am usually alone, and I allow this for myself. And then, as I used to tell my girls, 'I put on my big girl pants' and move on to something which puts a smile on my face.[10]

Chatting to another reader I discovered three very different experiences from three different sources of grief. Having lost both parents to dementia, she suggested to her husband that they went to a well-known UK prayer and retreat centre – Ffald y brenin.[11]

She described it like this:

> We went into the chapel. There is a rock in this chapel with a cross on it and after a couple of worship gatherings which we attended, I spent time at the foot of that cross on my own, howling. Up to that point I didn't know what to do with my

> feelings. There was a mixture. There was relief and gratitude that my parents were being spared, and that finally my mum and dad were home. But then at the same time I felt guilty of feeling relieved, and I didn't want it to be like that. Somehow during this process God gave me the ability to put him uppermost. It was as if my heart was saying, 'This is your will. I'm not very happy about it, in fact I hate it, but I can thank you in it.' That was a turning point for me. I found God in the midst of grief and God was then uppermost. It wasn't that the pain went, or all the grief disappeared, but the ability to handle it was different. I was no longer dragged under or dragged down by grief.

This same reader then shared about a miscarriage.

> I had a miscarriage, losing the baby at home. Because I was a midwife, I dealt with it, including dealing with the placenta myself. Then I just got up and cooked a meal. When it came time that evening for my youngest to go to bed, I laid down with her because at that age she didn't like to start going off to sleep on her own. I was able to say to God, 'I hate this, it hurts, but I trust you only do good things for me. Thank you!' And at that moment grace came, all on the same day. I found

myself only able to be truly soft in the presence of God. I still cry about losing the little baby who we called Deborah. The name is full of life and joy, and I know that where she is now, she is full of life enjoying heaven. God's will I know is always for the good, and 'thank you' stops the bitterness, stops grief dragging you down. 'I hate this!' – that's honesty. But I also say, 'Thank you.' And that's where God becomes uppermost, bitterness is dealt with and disabling grief is released.

As a nurse I also had long-term grief. I discovered that I had been grieving for many patients. On one occasion driving back from a church gathering where somehow my grief got stirred, my husband encouraged me to talk about it. Because we were going home to our kids, I knew that I couldn't handle it there and then. Over the following days, my husband insisted that I began to share – including the grief I was carrying for the relatives that I had had to deliver 'bad news' to.

A church member had a prophetic picture of me carrying a huge heavy tray, a really unmanageable heavy tray, and saw a load of cups and implements on this tray. Then a hand came from heaven. I expected the hand to take the tray from me, but no, the hand took one cup at a time. God took one thing at a time, and it reminded me that

> you can't carry the grief of others, only God can. Other people's grief can break your heart, but if we can find a way to let him, God will take it in manageable portions and, in time and over time, heal our hearts.[12]

The damage of anger

Of course, it is the case that for Joel's family in particular the loss has profound impact in multiple ways. On my own journey of grief, I have faced moments of irrepressible and intense anger. I first became aware of it when we came to the point where Joel's business had to be sold. I had a vested interest in the business, and it was a dark day for me, when during Covid restrictions I had to sit in a bleak, clinically clean office socially distanced from any human compassion or understanding and put my signatures to a paper that finalised the transaction of selling my son's business. Joel's family had had to face the same loss. However, processing this – the loss of my world, the loss of my income, the loss of my investment, the loss of my planned future dreams – led me to deeply and unhelpfully reacting. For around two weeks I had a barely restrained, barely constrained anger. I would keep revisiting the pain, venting to God himself and others, until one day God spoke very clearly to me from a conversation he had with Moses.

You may recall the story. Moses was dismayed that he couldn't enter the promised land – his dream. In relating an encounter with God, Moses says:

> But because of you the LORD was angry with me and would not listen to me. 'That is enough,' the LORD said. 'Do not speak to me any more about this matter.'[13]

It was the first and only time where God has spoken in quite that way. It resolved that one particular issue, and I have not had to face that specific issue again. However, the process exposed deeply buried anger. As I was to discover, that potential for anger still lurks, albeit somewhat buried, ready to surface at other moments.

Some years later we had a very difficult set of circumstances the outcome of which was that Gill and I faced unwanted and unexpected relational loss. I found myself being forced to make decisions which I would far rather have avoided, and in the process that intense anger surfaced again in one or two of the conversations I had and in emails I wrote. That anger was deeply damaging to those involved and I deeply regret that. I have endeavoured to put things right, but damage was done. The issue was not whether I was right or wrong in my decisions, but the unhelpful anger that spilled out of me along the way.

I had this explained to me by a friend who was studying trauma coaching:

> Your implicit memory (unconscious/automatic) holds memories that often have no language attached to them or awareness – lots of stuff we do every day uses this type of memory, for example, walking. But also, things we don't purposely try to remember. This is the area where 'triggers' are stored – sights, sounds, smells, or thoughts – that remind you of the trauma in some way. When these occur, your body prepares for fight/flight. Some of these triggers can activate PTSD symptoms so that you feel you're right back there. One such fight response is anger and the physiological responses that accompany it.
>
> Traumatic grief is when the intensity of grief is overwhelming or persistent/chronic, and so the grief itself becomes traumatic, as well as the sudden/traumatic events that preceded the grieving.
>
> Anger then is a natural response to a feeling of injustice or unfairness.

On the same evening as the conversation with my friend, Gill and I were watching *The West Wing*, the TV series. In that night's episode, the deputy chief of staff had been through an intense trauma and in the episode was inappropriately and outrageously speaking with great anger, challenging the President over things he was doing. In the programme, the storyline explored his trauma, and the unresolved nature of that trauma was to express itself in intense anger in a shockingly inappropriate way.

The three things together, signing away my son's business and God's response; the counselling input and the TV episode all helped me see the source of my anger, and has given me a pathway to lay it before God.

Scripture tells us it's OK to be angry, but with a weighty caveat: 'Be angry and do not sin; do not let the sun go down on your anger'.[14] Anger is a God-given emotion that God himself reflects. Anger is a mirror into the pain I have endured. And what I do with that will either cause damage to me and others, or will allow me to take a breath, unpack my anger with the 'Father of compassion and the God of all comfort'[15] and let the healing of that eternal comfort and compassion do its work.

Forgiving God

If there is a barrier to rebuilding and finding a place where God becomes uppermost, bitterness is dealt with and disabling grief is released, then unforgiveness will be in that mix.

People often ask about forgiving God. On a strictly theological level, that's impossible because God doesn't do anything wrong. However, there is a pragmatic way of viewing this. Forgiveness is about 'letting go' and, in this context, acknowledging where we may be holding something against God in our loss. Gill put it this way: 'I wrestled with the fact that God hadn't actually done anything wrong, so did I need to forgive? But then thinking about it, I realised I was holding it against God that he had taken Joel away. So, I prayed a simple, "I forgive you." As easy as that.' She felt different, something has lifted off her and since that moment, flashbacks, which were a common recurrence, have lessened.

> Forgiveness is giving up the hope that the past could have been any different, it's accepting the past for what it was, and using this moment and this time to help yourself move forward.[16]

As another reader, Lisa Voightmann, wrote:

> We suddenly lost our sweet twelve-year-old daughter in March 2017 to a brain haemorrhage. The grief was thick for quite some time. As a homeschool mother-of-three, I now had two grieving children to attend to, as well as a loving husband. I realised that I had a choice to make – I could let depression take me down to a dark place, or I could choose to release her to the Lord

> and keep living for my family and others. After some time, I also tried to thank God for the twelve wonderful years that we had with her, rather than cursing God for what we didn't have. This is a posture that has kept me sane and still loving my Lord. We know we will see her again and until then we keep seeking our Saviour – knowing that he's holding her and comforting us.

Grief is a very personal emotion, and we all handle it differently, but I truly believe that my faith has enabled me to overcome the grief and focus on the positives that these amazing people brought to my life. For all of that I shall be eternally grateful.

Forgiving others

For some, finding God in the journey of grief will involve forgiving others. Unforgiveness is a trap, easy to fall into, and once we are in there, the darkness can be overwhelming. There are so many ways in which during the sickness and dying of our loved ones, and the days that follow, we can find deep offences that if left will grow like weeds into large plants of bitterness or resentment, strangling the life out of any attempt to find a place of peace with God.

Forgiveness is often misunderstood. The word in Scripture means to 'let it go' or to 'cancel a debt'. Some people feel that if they forgive, then it means that the offence was not that bad. We may feel that if we forgive, the issue is no longer important or that we should not be sad. If the wrong was against someone we love, we may feel that as we forgive, we are betraying them.

But forgiveness never trivialises the offence.

In practical terms, forgiveness doesn't mean you are saying it doesn't matter. Forgiveness does not mean you are saying that 'what was done to me is OK'. Forgiveness acknowledges the full extent of the debt and then chooses to cancel it, chooses to release it. It is a conscious decision to let go of the hurt that the other person has caused.

Forgiveness unlocks the door to release the torment within us. It is the key to allowing the wound to heal. In doing so, God becomes uppermost, bitterness is dealt with and disabling grief is released.

It can be doctors, nurses and carers who let down our loved one in some way. Maybe there was a delay that cost life. Perhaps there was a misdiagnosis. If it's a suicide, it may be forgiving the loved one who died from suicide. In the case of an accident – forgiving the person who had caused it (maybe in a car accident) or even the one who died, if it was through their own carelessness. In the case of murder – forgiving the murderer. Forgiving yourself if you felt in any way guilty for what happened. In some cases, you might even feel angry with the person who has died for leaving you behind. Whatever it is, finding a place of forgiveness in your heart will bring release. Cancelling the debt, not holding it against another, is a key to healing, a key to the possibility of rebuilding.

Corrie Ten Boom writes: 'Forgiveness is the key that unlocks the door of resentment and the handcuffs of hatred. It is a power that breaks the chains of bitterness and the shackles of selfishness.'[17]

So that . . .

Earlier I mentioned two friends who in the middle of their grief were told, 'Now you've got your life message!' The inference being, 'God has allowed your grief in order to do something new through you.'

Let me say this as clearly as I am able, God hasn't taken Joel in order that I can find a new direction or purpose in God. That notion would trivialise his death and would cause untold damage to others who mourn his loss. However, there is an inference in one scripture that gives us some helpful clarity. In the grief of my loss God has promised:

> Praise be to the God and Father of our Lord Jesus Christ, the Father of compassion and the God of all comfort, who comforts us in all our troubles, so that we can comfort those in any trouble with the comfort we ourselves receive from God.[18]

You clocked it I'm sure: 'so that'.

Joel's death isn't the door, but my comfort from God is a door that opens up the possibility for me to serve others with comfort in any trouble. Why was it that during our *All About Heaven* evening events, hundreds of people would go out of their way to talk to us about their grief? Because they could sense the comfort of God manifest in our lives.

We mentioned Job earlier, and the scripture puts it this way: '[God] restored the fortunes of Job, when he had prayed for his friends.'[19] There is something empowering, God-honouring when we are able to reach out to others with the comfort we have received.

As one reader put it:

> I now use my experience of how God is close to the broken-hearted to encourage and strengthen others, which not only helps the people I share my story with, but it also helps and strengthens me as I share it.
>
> I can honestly say, I've never felt the presence of God more closely than walking this journey of grief.[20]

After the shocking and unexpected sudden death of his twenty-one-year-old son Nick, Tim Challies articulates the same notion like this:

I'm not the same man I was when Nick was alive. I'm deeply wounded, deeply scarred, deeply broken. Yet I know it is God who decreed this suffering, and I accept it as something meaningful, something precious, something sacred. I accept it as training for a ministry he has called me to. I'm ready to learn and to apply its lessons, painful though they may be. I know I'll be made better by it, made kinder, gentler, more empathetic more sanctified, and more useful. I know God has not called me away from duty but toward a new duty. He has not interrupted my usefulness to Him but has redirected it. And where He leads, I must follow. Where He leads, I will follow.[21]

Not Done Yet.

DOUBT, has not yet 'gate-crashed.'
Not yet anyway.
Joy and Truth are reliably intact and
darkness has not overcome The Light.
Questions are bound to be asked about
one's Faith.
If you believe in God
why have you have been so violently handled,
roughed over
so badly beaten up?
There is an answer, but tis only answered
through Silence.

Yet,
even with THIS Death,
THIS faith . . . has not stopped moving forward.
I'm Not Done Yet

Anthony L. Kelton

The rebuilding process doesn't wipe away tears. That promise is yet to come. I really do endeavour to continue to seek first the kingdom,[22] but I do so with wounds that this side of heaven will never truly heal. As Watchman Nee suggests, 'To keep your hand on the plow while wiping away our tears – THAT is Christianity!'[23]

My heart has been broken and my life is changed. But it is definitely not over. I do walk with a painful limp, but I still walk well. If I trust you, I may let you close enough for you to see the scars. And I am trusting the 'Father of compassion', the Father who genuinely 'in all things . . . works for the good of those who love him',[24] that through my grief and the authentic, incontrovertible comfort I have received, I will indeed keep moving forward.

And somewhere in that mix in my moving forward, my grief will prove to be a conduit for his will, his work, his way.

Our prayer for you

It may be today, it may be many years from now, but one thing is sure, certain and inescapable. There will be a moment when you find yourself or your loved ones walking through the valley of deepest darkness.

For that day and for that moment here is our prayer for you:

> May you lean into the trustworthy, wraparound
> love of the 'Father of compassion and the God of
> all comfort'.
> As you mourn, may you perceive his promised
> comfort in a multiplicity of ways.
> May you reach out and let him take you by the
> hand and guard you.
> May you find that lovingkindness that is better
> than life.
> In your broken-heartedness and when your spirit
> feels overwhelmed by sadness and crushed by
> the weight of loss . . . may you sense his promised
> closeness.
> May you find strength to keep your hand on the
> plough even as you wipe away your tears.
> We see your pain.
>
> *David and Gill*

Appendix One

Grief Online and the Digital Afterlife

Based on the premise that virtually every reader will have some form of online interaction and also use digital communications including texting, photos, WhatsApp, Facebook, Instagram or X, it's important that we do at least cover some positive and negative issues that will need addressing. It's especially important to think about the online world through the lens of every family member, and what is good and right and helpful for them.

In the online world, grief is collective. It's interesting that this varies dramatically. So, for example, in South Asia and in Jewish cultures, illness is mostly not spoken about. Here in the UK, we have a number of high-profile online influencers talking about dying, death and a proliferation in the UK and USA, especially of people sharing their grief on Instagram and Facebook. In the UK, Olympic champion Sir Chris Hoy has intentionally opened up the conversation around his terminal prostate cancer.[1] For a while the Bowel Babe[2] was prolific in raising awareness of bowel cancer and courageously documenting a journey through sickness and the final hours, to help others.

And on one level, the online world can make it attractively easier to share grief. You can explore a hashtag and find other groups of people that have been through what you've been through. If you want to, or if you find it helpful or cathartic, social media platforms allow you to share your journey and your grief. It's not always easy to do this in the real world, and support is not always easy to find there. The ability to turn it on or off at any time of night or day as the moment dictates can also be attractive.

It will be different for everyone, but do remember that ultimately, however helpful the online world is, it will be a superficial substitute for real human interaction.

It was interesting to me that in the early months, especially when Gill would find it hard to sleep and flashbacks were an unwelcome and regular visitor, she would turn to social media. Her logic was clear and thoughtful. She said to me, 'There are bound to be others who are going through worse experiences than us, and if I share in their story online, I can pray for them and do some good.'

Tips on social media usage, including prayer cover

If your loved one is ill, please ensure that you and they have talked about the use of social media. Some families like to share online with everyone. Many families, possibly most, want nothing on social media. In our case, Joel wanted to keep everything confidential, not least to protect his family from the impact of inappropriate or damaging information.

This is particularly important to remember when your mind is in a whirl from caring, making regular trips to the hospital or the hospice. It's easy to post something or send something by email or WhatsApp and discover it has given more information than other members of the family really wanted. Remember, too, the impact on children. Their friends may well see an Instagram or Facebook post and be telling them things about their dying mum, or dad, or relative that they didn't need to know or frankly shouldn't know.

Every family has different dynamics. My strong advice is: Please ensure that you chat this through, and agree on what is shared. Even if you are sharing for prayer cover, which for us was an essential support, check with the family and then be sure to let everyone know this is private and confidential and not to be shared on social media.

I made the mistake of posting what I thought were tender, thoughtfully crafted expressions of grief. They were highly personal, and I felt like they were honouring. But I didn't check and while some of our family liked the posts, others found them unwelcome, even distressing.

Taking pictures and collecting pictures

If there's one thing I've learned from grief, it is to take pictures. Take pictures of everything, everywhere of every single person you love and every single family member. Because at some point that's one of the most precious and memorable sources of memories. A simple way for you and others, family and friends, to stay close to the loved one.

What can help here is to consider an online book of remembrance.

Creating an online memorial page

It's fairly common in the UK and US to have a book of remembrance at the 'viewing' in the US and at the funeral or Thanksgiving Service in both the UK and US. Of course, lots of people who cannot get to the Thanksgiving Service, or the cremation, would like to have the opportunity to say something honouring or memorable.

Creating an online book of remembrance or memorial page, then, is a meaningful way to honour a loved one, allowing friends and family to share memories, condolences and tributes. Here's an overview of how these platforms work.

What is an online book of remembrance?

An online book of remembrance is a digital space where individuals can commemorate someone who has passed away. These platforms often allow users to:

- Post messages of condolence
- Share photographs and videos
- Light virtual candles or send virtual flowers
- Provide funeral details and RSVP options
- Collect charitable donations in memory of the deceased

Before any comments or posts are 'accepted', you or another family member have the opportunity to 'moderate' what goes public. These online books of remembrance can be shared via email or social media, making them accessible to a wide audience.

Many funeral services will offer this service and there are also a plethora of online services that offer a whole range of inexpensive packages. It has the added advantage that people are able to upload their pictures of your loved one, giving you a raft of new images to enjoy.

Key Search tip: Simply type into Google or ChatGPT: 'How to Create an Online Memorial'

Saving messages, emails, photos and recordings

Preserving all text messages and WhatsApp messages from a deceased loved one can be deeply important and comforting.

Also make sure phones, iPads and computers are backed up. You may also want to think about printing out all or some emails.

If it's possible, before your loved one dies, make sure their phone has a designated recovery contact or a legacy contact. This can save untold stress and heartache if you can't get into your loved one's phone (or computer).

This all comes with a health warning. Looking through emails and photos, or viewing or listening to video or audio can be deeply impacting. My point being, be kind to yourself and be alert to the inevitable grief trigger.

It's worth thinking and intentionally chatting through with family members about the possible memories to be distributed among family. In our case, we had multiple audio recordings which Joel was keen for us to make. I set aside a day or two to listen to every recording and give each one a name with a brief abstract of what the content was. My intent was simply to make it easy for any family member to listen to whatever they chose. The emotional impact was unexpectedly brutal and lasted for a couple of weeks. We know there will be tripwires or triggers, and yet still they can catch us out.

Key Search tip: Simply type into Google or ChatGPT: 'Setting up a recovery contact or legacy contact'

Watch out for your own Facebook or Instagram posts

I was busy and absent-mindedly tapping away on Facebook yesterday. Several birthdays came up and as is my habit most days, I posted *Happy Birthday* to several on the prompted list. An hour or so later I got a WhatsApp message from a friend asking if I had forgotten that one lady had died two years before. I went hot and cold thinking of her family and the pain it might cause them. So I immediately checked online how to delete a birthday post.

Key Search tip: You can type into Google or ChatGPT: 'How to remove a post' or 'How to remove a post on someone else's timeline'

Online triggers of grief

Regularly Facebook pops up anniversary posts 'this time ten years ago' or 'this day two years ago' and those reminders can either bring out-of-the-blue brutal moments of grief, or unexpected tears, or warm gratitude for the memories. It's just one more thing on the journey to expect and be prepared for.

One of the big tear-jerkers for me was the first time I used 'Find My' on my iPhone. Up came my list of names of friends and family members and their current location. Right at the bottom was Joel Oliver: 'No location found'.

Appendix Two

Bereavement Care Checklist

This checklist is designed to help church leaders (and other pastoral workers, including family and carers) provide compassionate, comprehensive care to grieving families, loved ones and friends following a death. It would help too if each member of the team or those who are involved could read chapters six and seven: Help That Hurts and Help That Heals.

Please remember this is never about you and how you feel, but always about those who mourn. 'Please give me space and leave me alone' would not be the same for someone who says, 'Please come, I need you around.'

Whatever the circumstances when it comes to church care and response, *time* is the greatest gift you can offer. It won't necessarily always be accepted so be prepared for that. However, any kind of rush communicates 'checklist care' not 'care from the heart'. And please do also remember you will get some things wrong and some things right and that's OK. You don't have to be perfect, just present. Maybe at every stage, like my friend Rob Parsons, you can pray, 'Lord, let me do them no harm.'

Initial contact (within twenty-four hours).

Express condolences with compassion and empathy.

Offer prayer and spiritual comfort.

Ask if the family would like a visit or phone call. Ensure they know you are available and present.

Practical and logistical support

Ask if they would like a funeral or memorial service at the church.

Leave care packages.

Offer guidance on planning the service (readings, music, tributes).

Coordinate with funeral directors (if requested).

Assist with any paperwork or liaise with other churches if needed.

Offer help for immediate practical needs (for example, meals, childcare, transportation). Please be specific about exactly how you can help so they know what's on offer.

Ensure key church staff/volunteers are informed and available. Agree with prayer on your leadership team who is the best person to be most involved.

Pastoral care for the bereaved

Identify the closest next of kin and maintain sensitive contact. In particular, agree what kind and level of input is needed for each family member. And please remember: Children, especially if they are siblings of the deceased, are often the most forgotten mourners.

Offer pastoral visits or calls in the days and weeks following the death.

Encourage openness about grief – don't rush them. Remember to talk about their loved one, give them space to talk about them too. And LET THEM CRY!

Help them navigate faith and questions around death, suffering and hope. You will find this uncomfortable and so will they. Some helpful resources can be found in the Bibliography and Resources.

Funeral or memorial service

Be aware of any request or wishes already prepared by the loved one, and agree who in the family is the contact point.

Check if they would like you to meet with the whole family face to face, online or a combination.

Help the family agree together a service that honours the deceased and comforts the living. You may discover some tensions in this phase so be prepared.

Ensure involvement from the family if they want, in readings, tributes, or music.

Provide a short, meaningful message of hope and resurrection wherever that's appropriate. And do agree the nature of your message with the family, especially if some members have no faith.

Confirm logistics: timing, AV needs, music, seating, livestream if needed.

Offer to lead or assist with the service, burial or cremation.

Support for wider circle (friends, church members)

Inform the congregation (respecting privacy and family wishes).

Keep regular prayer cover in place and agree with family the extent of communication and ensure they are happy, e.g. with email and WhatsApp for prayer pointers and updates.

Provide a space for people to grieve together (service, vigil, prayer gathering).

Encourage church community to reach out to the family. Where you can, give practical guidance. Where it's helpful, maybe even give a few copies of this book pointing to a specific, relevant chapter to make it easy.

Make pastoral support available for others affected (friends, youth, elderly).

Ongoing follow-up (weeks and months later)

Talk about this and agree the following with your leadership team:

Schedule pastoral check-ins at key intervals (one month, three months, six months, one year).

Acknowledge significant dates (birthday, anniversary of death, Christmas Thanksgiving). For each of these dates, pray and talk through what practical support you might offer.

Invite them where it's appropriate to grief support groups, counselling or prayer gatherings.

Provide resources on grief (books, leaflets, podcasts, Scripture). But only when you are sure it's appropriate. 'Offer' this rather than 'propose' this.

Remind them they are not forgotten, and the church still cares.

Please remember that many cannot or do not read – even Scripture – so be aware of that when offering books (even mine!) or the Bible. Find out what helps each individual and help as practically as you can.

Be alert to signs of intense or complicated grief and refer to counselling if needed.

Spiritual encouragement

Share Scripture, prayer and words of comfort, YouTube clips appropriately.

Speak of hope in Christ, the resurrection and the promise of eternal life. And (only when it's appropriate) if you are able gift a copy of *All About Heaven*[1] and/or link them to the live recording of the *All About Heaven* evening event https://bit.ly/AAHOX1

Encourage reflection, journaling or prayer for some as part of the grieving process.

Offer personal prayer ministry if appropriate.

Administrative and communication

Keep a private pastoral record of contact and support offered.

Ensure the death is noted in church records and communications (with family consent).

Add the bereaved to your pastoral care or prayer list for ongoing follow-up.

All About Grief

Your Church Can Host the Evening Event

David & Gill Oliver share from their heart, the trauma, the grief, the hope & the insights that surrounded and subsequently followed the tragic death of Joel, their eldest son, just seventeen days after the diagnosis of a brutal cancer.

After Joel's death, David researched and then wrote the bestselling book *All About Heaven*. He and Gill have spoken at twenty-nine evening events by the same name in the USA and UK.

During these evening events, David writes, 'Again and again we were surprised by the number of people who would come up to Gill and me after the event, not to talk about heaven but to talk about their grief. It was almost as if they were wanting to give their loved one a voice. And in the process, indicating they had been unable to do this in their church settings. This birthed the desire to write this new book *All About Grief*.'

Answering the most common questions around grief, this new book is a trusted companion for those grieving and a practical guide for those who comfort them.

Grief is a universal experience and with the loss of a partner, a parent, a child or a friend the impact is profound and personal. Yet for an experience apparently so common, it can be incredibly lonely. People often don't know what to say. The world around you seems to move on while your own world has stopped. Faith at times can feel so desperately fragile. Others want you to 'move on', they want to 'fix the pain.'

All About Grief (two 45-minute sessions, with a 15-minute break) can be hosted at your church as an evening event (in person or online) and will explore how we can live through the most debilitating, shocking and dark moments of loss without losing hope.

Each session gently helps listeners understand the journey they are on, and then helps them find some measure of hope when life feels broken beyond repair. Drawing on personal experience, interviews and years of speaking and writing about life, loss and hope, *All About Grief* the evening event will help attendees make sense of their emotions; process their pain and take small steps towards healing.

Hosting an event is easy. All the template materials for easy promotion are supplied to your church, free of charge. This includes two promotional videos, a bulletin, newsletter text, a promotional flyer and social media content.

To find out more, go to https://davidoliverbooks.com/pages/host-an-event or scan the QR code at the bottom of this page.

Free PDF Resources for Readers

For a free PDF version of the Bereavement Care Checklist, please email david@davidoliverbooks.com

For a free PDF containing a full list of scriptures on expressions of grief and mourning, please email david@davidoliverbooks.com

For a free PDF covering various models of grief, please email david@davidoliverbooks.com

Bibliography and Resources

All About Heaven by David Oliver (www.davidoliverbooks.com)

The deepest question in life is, 'What happens when I die?' I am grateful for *All About Heaven* as it lifts my eyes, heart and mind to another world more real than this one.

Rob Parsons, OBE, founder and chair, Care for the Family

Every Christian should read this book.

David Pawson, international Bible teacher

To view *All About Heaven*, the evening event from a live recording in Oxford, UK: https://bit.ly/AAHOX1

Books

Tim Challies, *Seasons of Sorrow: The Pain of Loss and the Comfort of God* (Grand Rapids, MI: Zondervan, 2022)

Barney Coombs, *A Guide to Practical Pastoring* (Eastbourne, Kingsway Publications: Sovereign World International, 1993)

John Ellwood, A Journey Through Cancer (Welwyn Garden City: Malcolm Down Publishing, 2020)

Roger Greene, Dancing When the Lights Go Out (Welwyn Garden City: Malcolm Down Publishing, 2024)

C.S. Lewis, *A Grief Observed* (London: Faber & Faber, 2013)

Chimamanda Ngozi Adichie, *Notes on Grief* (London: Fourth Estate, 2021)

Rob Parsons, *A Knock at the Door: A New Story of Hope* (London: Hodder & Stoughton, 2019)

John Wyatt, *Dying Well* (London: IVP, 2018)

Websites

Louise Blyth, Hope is Coming, www.yellowkitebooks.co.uk/titles/louise-blyth/hope-is-coming/9781529395532/?

Sarah Rowlands and Claire Musters, 'The Grief Journey', Care for the Family, www.careforthefamily.org

Yvonne Tulloch, *Faith Questions in Bereavement*, www.thebereavementjourney.org

Where can I turn to for help with grief, even traumatic grief?

Gill and I have spent some time researching various options that are available to help folk with their grieving journey. We can offer the following list. Each option would need each individual to evaluate whether this was a helpful fit.

Originally based out of Holy Trinity Brompton (HTB), available in UK for church use, is a bereavement counselling course run on a similar model to Alpha and suitable for those with and those without a faith: www.ataloss.org

Equipping churches for bereavement support:
www.lossandhope.org

Recommended to us as a Christian counselling service in the UK, recommended by the British and Foreign Bible Society: www.willowscounselling.org.uk

Available in the UK and USA from the Bible Society:
www. traumahealinginstitute.org/groups

Available in the UK and USA:
www. sanctuarymentalhealth.org/when-a-loved-one-dies-by-suicide/

www.sanctuarymentalhealth.org/about-faith-grief-and-covid-19/

Endnotes

Introduction

1. Welwyn Garden City: Malcolm Down Publishing, 2020.

Chapter One

1. Benjamin Franklin, *Letter to Jean-Baptiste Leroy*, 13 November 1789. In *The Papers of Benjamin Franklin*, vol. 43, ed. William B. Willcox (New Haven, CT: Yale University Press), p. 69.
2. Day 272: 'Two Universal Appointments', part of his *Foundations* series on the Derek Prince Ministries website, www.derekprince.com/devotionals/c-b052-272?(accessed 1.10.25).
3. Roger Greene, *Dancing When the Lights Go Out* (Welwyn Garden City: Malcolm Down Publishing, 2024), p. 153.
4. Ecclesiastes 3:2; 7:2
5. 1 Corinthians 15:3.
6. Hebrews 6:1–3.
7. 1 Thessalonians 4:13.
8. I Thessalonians 4:18.
9. No verifiable source available for this quote but it follows the first law of thermodynamics.
10. Burris Jenkins. It appears in his essay, 'Life Persistently Triumphs by Burris Jenkins', included in Thomas Curtis Clark and Hazel David Clark (eds), *The Golden Book of Immortality: A Treasury of Testimony* (New York: Association Press, 1954).

11. 1 Corinthians 15:55.
12. Ecclesiastes 12:7.
13. Luke 23:43.
14. Isaiah 38:10 & 12, ESV
15. 2 Corinthians 5:1.
16. 2 Corinthians 4:16.
17. Philippians 1:23.
18. 2 Timothy 4:6.
19. See for example Matthew 17:1–13.
20. Acts 7:59–60.
21. Luke 23:46.
22. Acts 7:55.
23. Luke 8:52–55, my emphasis.
24. 2 Corinthians 5:6–8.
25. Philippians 1:21–24.
26. Luke 23:42–43; John 14:1–32; 2 Corinthians 5:6–8; 2 Corinthians 12:2–4; Revelation 2:7. See also 1 Peter 2:11, AMPC.
27. John 14:2.
28. Psalm 116:15–16.
29. John 14:28.
30. Revelation 14:13.
31. Psalm 116:15.

32. Quote from Elie Wiesel Nobel lecture, 11 December 1988, www.nobelprize.org/prizes/peace/1986/wiesel/lecture/?u (1.10.25).
33. Hebrews 2:9.
34. Hebrews 2:8,14–15, *The Message.*
35. Mother Teresa, www.armagharchdiocese.org/wp-content/uploads/2013/05/A-prayer-for-loss-and-Grief..pdf? (accessed 27.10.25).
36. Philippians 1:23.

Chapter Two

1. Paraphrasing Lee Child, *Tripwire* (London: Bantam, 2011).
2. Ecclesiastes 3:1–2.
3. Philippians 1:20–21, ESV.
4. Romans 14:7–8.
5. Spoken by Pope Francis during his General Audience on 16 June 2021, www.vatican.va/content/francesco/en/audiences/2021/documents/papa-francesco_20210616_udienza-generale.html? (accessed 1.10.25).
6. See Hebrews 13:5.
7. Edited for the purposes of this book.
8. See 2 Timothy 4:7.
9. See James 5:13–15.
10. Revelation 1:18.

11. See 2 Corinthians 12:8–9.
12. Psalm 63:3–4, NKJV.
13. See Romans 8:28.
14. Edited for the purposes of this book.

Chapter Three

1. Matthew 5:4.
2. Psalm 90:10, ASV (as found on www.BibleGateway.com).
3. 1 Thessalonians 4:13, ESV.
4. Taken from *Remember Heaven* by Matthew McCulloch © May 2025. Used by permission of Crossway, a publishing ministry of Good News Publishers, Wheaton, IL 60187, www.crossway.org.
5. Philippians 1:21.
6. Psalm 34:18.
7. Genesis 1:26.
8. See https://thingsabove.us/jesus-wept-but-not-for-lazarus/? (accessed 29.10.25).
9. John 11:33–36, ESV, my emphasis.
10. See John 19:26–27.
11. Matthew 14:13.
12. Bear Grylls, *The Greatest Story Ever Told* (London: Hodder Faith, 2025), p. 129.
13. Isaiah 53:3, ESV.
14. See Psalm 56:8, ESV.

15. Hebrews 4:15.
16. Lamentations 1:20; Lamentations 2:11; Lamentations 3:13; Jeremiah 4:19; Lamentations 2:19.
17. Psalm 31:9; Psalm 31:9–10; Psalm 102:4; Psalm 34:18; Psalm 6:6; Micah 1:8.
18. The NCB translation is the nearest: 'The heart knows its own grief best'.
19. Proverbs 15:11.
20. 1 Kings 8:39.
21. *Honoring Grief and Finding Meaning with David Kessler*, Episode 49, https://awcim.arizona.edu/podcast/episode49_kessler.html? (accessed 1.10.25).
22. Greene, *Dancing When the Lights Go Out*, p. 44.

Chapter Four

1. Source unfound.
2. Elisabeth Kübler-Ross, *On Death and Dying* (New York: Macmillan, 1969).
3. David Kessler, *Finding Meaning: The Sixth Stage of Grief*, www.goodreads.com/quotes/10094565-each-person-s-grief-is-as-unique-as-their-fingerprint-but? (accessed 1.10.25).
4. David Kessler, *Finding Meaning: The Sixth Stage of Grief*, www.goodreads.com/quotes/10094565-each-person-s-grief-is-as-unique-as-their-fingerprint-but? (accessed 1.10.25).
5. Edited for the purposes of this book.

6. Pat Smekal, *Let Grief: Healing Your Way Through Loss* (Vancouver: Douglas & McIntyre, 1990). No longer in print.
7. Sent as reader comments, some paraphrasing of Richard Littledale, *Postcards from the Land of Grief* (Milton Keynes: Authentic Media, 2019).
8. Edited for the purposes of this book.
9. Edited for the purposes of this book.
10. Edited for the purposes of this book.
11. Proverbs 25:20, NLT.
12. www.taps.org/articles/21-1/divorce/? (accessed 1.10.25).
13. 'Examining the Marital Relationship After the Death of a Child', https://journals.sagepub.com/doi/10.1177/10664807221104129 (accessed 24.9.25). S. Albuquerque, M. Pereira, I. Narciso (2016), 'Couple's relationship after the death of a child: A systematic review', *Journal of Child Family Studies*, 25, 30–53, https://link.springer.com/article/10.1007/s10826-015-0219-2 (accessed 1.10.25).
14. K. Cherry, 'What is complicated grief? Symptoms, diagnosis, and treatment', 4 January 2025, Verywell Mind, www.verywellmind.com/complicated-grief-symptoms-diagnosis-and-treatment-5089396 (accessed 20.10.25).

Chapter Five

1. Psalm 23:4, GNT.
2. See Luke 24:5.
3. Edited for the purposes of this book.

4. Melani Sessa, founder of @Grace_and_Grief_Healing.
5. Edited for the purposes of this book.

Chapter Six

1. *A Grief Observed* by CS Lewis © copyright 1961
   CS Lewis Pte Ltd. Extract used with permission
   Rachel Churchill
   The CS Lewis Company Ltd.
2. 1 Thessalonians 4:13.
3. See Psalm 56:8, ESV.
4. See Isaiah 61:3.
5. Ecclesiastes 3:4.
6. Edited for the purposes of this book.
7. Speaker/author: Nora McInerny TED talk, 'We don't "move on" from grief. We move forward with it', delivered at TEDWomen, filmed 28 November, 2018, www.youtube.com/watch?v=khkJkR-ipfw (accessed 1.10.25).
8. Extracts of examples from emails sent to us from readers of *All About Heaven*.

Chapter Seven

1. Edited for the purposes of this book.
2. Romans 12:15, ESV.
3. Edited for the purposes of this book.

4. Henri J.M. Nouwen, 1974. *Out of Solitude: Three Meditations on the Christian Life* (Notre Dame, IN: Ave Maria Press, 1974), https://www.azquotes.com/author/10905-Henri_Nouwen/tag/grieving? (accessed 20.10.25).
5. Kessler, *Finding Meaning: The Sixth Stage of Grief*, www.goodreads.com/quotes/10094565-each-person-s-grief-is-as-unique-as-their-fingerprint-but? (accessed 1.10.25).
6. Edited for the purposes of this book.
7. Greene, *Dancing When the Lights Go* Out, p. 39.
8. 2 Corinthians 7:6.

Chapter Eight

1. Yvonne Tulloch, *Faith Questions in Bereavement*, booklet from the Bereavement Course www.thebereavementjourney.org/store/p/the-bereavement-journey-guest-manual-tbj02-t5fys? (accessed 20.10.25).
2. Job 5:7.
3. Matthew 26:39, NLT.
4. Matthew 27:46.
5. 2 Corinthians 12:8–9.
6. James 5:14–15.
7. Hebrews 9:27.
8. Psalm 63:3, NKJV.
9. Luke 22:42.

10. Edited for the purposes of this book.
11. Revelation 1:18.
12. Ecclesiastes 8:8, ESV.
13. Matthew 6:33.
14. Elisabeth Elliot, *Secure in the Everlasting Arms* (Nashville, TN: Thomas Nelson, 2002).
15. Reprinted by permission of HarperCollins Publishers Ltd © 2024 Rob Parsons. P. 327.
16. See Luke 2:35.
17. Parsons, *A Knock at the Door: A New Story of Hope*, p. 327.

Chapter Nine

1. See Psalm 23.
2. Isaiah 42:6, NLT.
3. Source not found.
4. Psalm 34:18.
5. Psalm 147:3.
6. Isaiah 61:1.
7. 1 Corinthians 15:55, ESV.
8. Matthew 5:4.
9. Matthew 5:4.
10. See 1 Corinthians 12 about the spiritual gifts. Or see David Oliver, *Find Your Voice* (Milton Keynes: Authentic Publishing, 2007).

11. 2 Corinthians 7:6, AMPC.
12. Psalm 23:1.
13. Psalm 23:4, ESV.
14. Psalm 63:3, NKJV.
15. Job 1:21, NKJV.
16. Steven Curtis Chapman, *The Glorious Unfolding* (2013), Reunion Records; distributor Reunion Records and Sony Music.
17. Alfred, Lord Tennyson, 'Break, Break, Break'. Written in 1835, first published 1842.
18. Henry Alford (1810-71), *Ten Thousand Times Ten Thousand*, https://hymnary.org/text/ten_thousand_times_ten_thousand_in_spark? (accessed 1.10.25).
19. 2 Corinthians 1:3.
20. Romans 8:15–16.
21. 2 Corinthians 1:3.
22. Philippians 1:23, ESV.
23. 1 Corinthians 2:9, ESV.
24. *The Last Battle* by CS Lewis © copyright 1956 CS Lewis Pte Ltd.

Chapter Ten

1. Elie Wiesel Nobel Prize lecture, www.nobelprize.org/prizes/peace/1986/wiesel/lecture/ (accessed 29.9.25).

2. Genesis 35:19.
3. Genesis 30:1.
4. Genesis 30:24.
5. Genesis 35:18.
6. Genesis 29:20.
7. Genesis 37:34–35.
8. Job 1:21, ESV.
9. Edited for the purposes of this book.
10. Edited for the purposes of this book.
11. https://ffald-y-brenin.org (accessed 29.9.25).
12. Edited for the purposes of this book.
13. Deuteronomy 3:26.
14. Ephesians 4:26, ESV.
15. 2 Corinthians 1:3.
16. Oprah Winfrey, 2021 article on Oprah Daily, www.oprahdaily.com/life/a37117486/oprah-forgiveness/? (accessed 1.10.25).
17. Corrie Ten Boom, *Tramp for the Lord* (Fort Washington, PA: CLC Publications, 2008, www.goodreads.com/quotes/7296327-forgiveness-is-the-key-which-unlocks-the-door-of-resentment? (accessed 1.10.25).
18. 2 Corinthians 1:3–4.
19. Job 42:10, ESV.
20. Edited for the purposes of this book.

21. Taken from *Seasons of Sorrow: The Pain of Loss and the Comfort of God* by Tim Challies Copyright © 2022 by Tim Challies. Used by permission of HarperCollins Christian Publishing. www.harpercollinschristian.com
22. See Matthew 6:33.
23. https://quotefancy.com/quote/932083/Watchman-Nee-To-keep-our-hand-on-the-plow-while-wiping-away-our-tears-THAT-is (accessed 29.9.25).
24. Romans 8:28.

Appendix One

1. 'Olympic Champion Sir Chris Hoy: Living With Incurable Cancer', www.youtube.com/watch?v=dkaZmbWUDWA, first Broadcast 10.12.24 (accessed 1.10.25).
2. 'Deborah James the 'Bowel Babe' Thought Her Bowel Cancer Was IBS', www.youtube.com/watch?v=MGMy6BzBvp0 (accessed 29.9.25).

Appendix Two

1. www.davidoliverbooks.com (accessed 29.9.25).

All About Grief

Bulk Purchase Discount

for small groups church distribution or for family and friends

It's possible you would like to invest in this message by purchasing multiple copies for family and friends, small group study or large-scale church distribution. We want to make this easy and simple and say 'thank you' by helping you to keep your costs down.

Please select from the options below.

UK and USA BULK PRICING

For deep discounts on 5, 10, 50 or 100 copies and more visit the page below

https://davidoliverbooks.com/collections/all-about-grief-bulk-purchasing

NB For larger bulk buy discounts or for sale or return policy for churches please use the contact form at www.davidoliverbooks.com to enquire

Also by David Oliver

ISBN: 978-1-912863-24-2

What happens when we die? What does heaven look like? What will occupy us there? When David Oliver faced the death of his son Joel, at the age of 38, following a short and brutal fight with cancer, he set about researching and writing this powerful short book on heaven and committed to write whatever he discovered.

The deepest question in life is 'What happens when I die?' and yet there are few books today that grapple with that issue. I am grateful for *All About Heaven* – it lifts my eyes, heart and mind to another world – more real than this one.

Rob Parsons, OBE, Founder & Chairman, Care for the Family,

This book is tremendous and should be read by all Christians

David Pawson, International Bible Teacher,

Available www.davidoliverbooks.com

www.ingramcontent.com/pod-product-compliance
Lightning Source LLC
LaVergne TN
LVHW020043110826
845155LV00029B/612